Contents

THE PILL

An Essential Guide

613.943

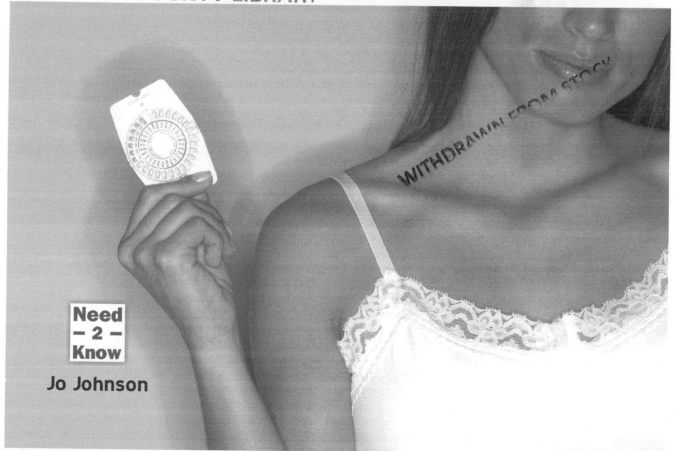

**Need
– 2 –
Know**

Jo Johnson

First published in Great Britain in 2008 by
Need2Know
Remus House
Coltsfoot Drive
Peterborough
PE2 9JX
Telephone 01733 898103
Fax 01733 313524
www.need2knowbooks.co.uk

Need2Know is an imprint of Forward Press Ltd.
www.forwardpress.co.uk
SB ISBN 978-1-86144-058-7
Cover photograph: Jupiter Images

Introduction

The need for contraception is now more important than ever before. It is no secret that young women and teenagers are having more sexual partners at an earlier age and are failing to protect themselves against accidental and unwanted pregnancies. The figures for these statistics are repeatedly seen in magazines and newspaper headlines, raising two important questions: why is this happening and what can we do to prevent it?

Contraception and information about contraception is now easily accessed, but there still seems to be a lack of awareness regarding this subject, and a shortfall in the level of compliance once contraception has been issued. This book aims to address these issues and to alleviate some of the myths that surround the oral contraceptive, answering all the questions you were afraid to ask. Written by a nurse, the information is presented in a straightforward manner, without using complicated medical terminology.

As the title suggests, this book provides information about contraceptive methods, focussing in particular on the oral contraceptive pill. Included in this information is a detailed account of the variety of contraceptive pills available, which varieties are most suitable for different women, the benefits and disadvantages of each type of pill and how to use them properly to ensure that they are most effective.

In addition to this there is a section addressing the emergency contraceptive pill and information regarding the currently researched male oral contraceptive.

Importantly, this guide is not just aimed at young people. Modern women are now finding the challenges of balancing careers, finances and family issues increasingly difficult to juggle. By taking charge of your own fertility it is now possible to plan your life, to decide when the most opportune time to start a family will be and to control the timing between each subsequent pregnancy.

Written for both men and women of all ages throughout the UK, the guide can also be used as a useful reference tool for healthcare students and those wishing to build their knowledge of female oral contraceptives.

By the end of the book not only will you have gained a sound knowledge about the oral contraceptive pill, but you will be fully equipped with all the information needed to make an educated decision about which type of contraception is most suited to your health and which will fit most suitably into your lifestyle.

Disclaimer

This book is for general information about contraception and the pill. It is not intended to replace professional medical advice. It can be used alongside medical advice, but anyone thinking about taking the pill is strongly advised to consult their healthcare professional.

'Modern women are now finding the challenges of balancing careers, finances and family issues increasingly difficult to juggle.'

Whilst every care has been taken to validate the contents of this guide up to the time of going to press, the author advises that she does not claim medical qualifications. Readers should seek advice from a qualified medical practitioner before undertaking any particular course of treatment.

Chapter One

All About Contraception

What is contraception?

Contraception is a way of taking control of your fertility, providing you with protection against unplanned and unwanted pregnancies.

For most, it exists to prevent unplanned pregnancy, allowing people – women especially – the choice of deciding the right time to start a family. It may be that a family already has children and doesn't want or is not ready for anymore additions. Perhaps a woman wants to have children in the future, but at present is not emotionally, psychologically or financially ready to start a family.

Selecting an acceptable form of contraception can allow the liberty of continuing to enjoy a healthy sex life, preferably with the same partner for many years, without the worry of conception. Of course, this is providing the selected method is used correctly.

Contraception can also help to control the increasing population all around the globe and many groups of people, who in the past did not recognise or accept contraception, now understand the important role it can play in today's society.

Selecting a suitable form of contraception

Everyone has their own preference and choice regarding their likes, dislikes and lifestyle choices. Selecting a method of birth control is no different. When educated about the wide variety of contraception available, everyone will find they develop their own ideas about which type will fit their lifestyle in the most effective manner. However, making this decision is definitely made

'Selecting an acceptable form of contraception can allow the liberty of continuing to enjoy a healthy sex life, preferably with the same partner for many years, without the worry of conception.'

easier by being aware of all the facts associated with each different type of contraception available, knowing how to use them all efficiently and how to ensure their effectiveness.

The existing types of contraception available in the UK are varied and it can be somewhat overwhelming. As it is such an important subject, it is vital that you get some amount of knowledge about available methods in order to make a fully informed and educated selection in finding a method that is suitable to your individual needs.

There are several issues that may influence the selection of one form over another, or indeed choosing none at all. Factors that may influence contraceptive decisions may include religious and personal beliefs, your current physical health or past medical history, the types of sexual relationships you are planning and what services are offered in your region.

As you can see, there are many considerations to be thought about before a decision is made, all of which should be thoroughly researched before making a final choice.

'There are several issues that may influence the selection of one form over another, or indeed choosing none at all.'

Deciding on a method to suit your individual needs

Your circumstances will be different to those around you and you may find that a friend or relative's contraceptive choice would not fit with your lifestyle or preferences. The key point to remember is that you should make your own choice, without being influenced by others.

For example, a woman who works as an air stewardess is going to undergo long haul flights and will be frequently adjusting to time differences. As a result, she might not be able to manage with an oral contraceptive as it could prove too difficult to keep track of the times it needs to be taken, therefore an alternative method of birth control will probably prove to be more effective and easier to use.

If you are bad at keeping appointments, you may find that the commitment needed to take some forms of contraception, such as the injection, is too much. At worst, you could find that you have not got adequate contraceptive cover, which could result in an unplanned pregnancy.

Another contributory factor will be the advice provided by your healthcare provider as they will be able to determine which methods may or may not be suitable depending on your health status.

Whatever the reason, it is crucial that the type of contraception used is going to be suited to your own needs and requirements.

Protecting against sexually transmitted infections

All contraceptive methods aim to protect against unwanted pregnancies, but just as important is protecting against sexually transmitted infections or STIs (in the past these were known as sexually transmitted diseases or STDs, before which they were called venereal diseases, otherwise called VD).

As research and development has gained more knowledge about the infections, their causes and their transmission, the public are now better equipped than ever to protect against them. However, statistics continue to show that the incidence of many of these illnesses is increasing, despite methods of protection being so widely available and well publicised.

In modern society, people are having more casual sex with a greater number of sexual partners than previous generations. They are also not protecting their health. There are several possible explanations for this, including the increase in alcohol consumption, the generally accepted concept of one night only sexual encounters and sexual equality.

It cannot be stressed enough that protecting yourself from these diseases is essential to maintaining good health and protecting against some of the lesser known but long term consequences, such as infertility, pain and consequential infections.

Of all the methods that are available, only the male and female condom provides adequate protection against these disorders.

Couples who are in long term relationships (where both parties involved are sure that there is no risk of infection) may find that they no longer wish to use condoms and might find an alternative form of contraception. However, it is recommended that condoms are kept handy in case of a missed pill or other reasons that may decrease the effectiveness of the normally used

'Whatever the reason, it is crucial that the type of contraception used is going to be suited to your own needs and requirements.'

contraceptive. For many modern women though, using condoms is essential when a new partner is chosen or if they are likely to have a number of sexual partners.

Infections and their consequences

The types of infections and disorders that the condom can help protect from include HIV, which may lead to AIDS and early mortality, hepatitis, gonorrhoea, chlamydia, syphilis and herpes.

'In modern society, people are having more casual sex with a greater number of sexual partners than previous generations. They are also not protecting their health.'

If these diseases and infections are left undiagnosed and untreated, the effects can have a significant impact on physical health, emotional well-being, lifestyle and mental health.

Pain and discomfort commonly arise from many of the infections as they can spread throughout the pelvis and affect other organs and tissues. Infertility is just one of the possible outcomes that can result, rendering the person unable to have children or being forced to undergo lengthy and expensive fertility treatments. In worst cases, they can even result in death.

The more serious infections such as HIV often lead to lengthy treatments, surveillance and screening processes. Treatment options frequently include complicated drug regimes and changes in lifestyle which aim to prevent health deteriorating.

It is vital that when choosing a suitable form of birth control, the issues surrounding STIs are considered and appropriate forms of protection are sought. For more detailed information, check out *Sexually Transmitted Infections – The Essential Guide.*

Checklist

- Do I know about all the different types of contraception available?
- Do I have a basic knowledge of how they work?
- Which methods are most suitable to my lifestyle?
- Which methods protect against sexually transmitted infections?

Need2Know

Summing Up

Contraception is a method of protecting yourself from unplanned and often unwanted pregnancy by interfering or interception of the way in which a sperm fertilises an egg.

When selecting a form of contraception it is important to identify what your individual needs are, how they can be met and what types of contraception you would not feel comfortable using.

As every female is individual, the decision should be made independently once all the facts are known and a personal preference can be determined.

Consideration should also be given to the issues surrounding STIs as these are becoming increasingly more widespread, especially in younger generations.

Read *Sexually Transmitted Infections – The Essential Guide* for more information.

'It is vital that when choosing a suitable form of birth control, the issues surrounding STIs are considered and appropriate forms of protection are sought.'

Chapter Two

Types of Contraception

Why we need different forms of contraception

Living in today's modern society, with medical research developing new and improved solutions and treatments for a vast spectrum of health-related issues, provides the general public with more choices than ever before.

Although contraception is not a recent development, it has seen some significant advances in the past few decades and there is now such a wide range of products available that everyone should be able to find a form that suits their needs.

Apart from the contraceptive pill, there are many other types of birth control that are available for general use. It is important that there is a good variety of contraceptive measures available, because by providing more options, the likelihood of compliancy and people requesting and using contraception increases. It also gives you more choice!

It may be that one or more particular varieties are not suitable for your needs; perhaps one type cannot be used because of health reasons, is not a preferred method of your choice or you know and understand more about one type than another. It really doesn't matter which type you choose, as long as it is suitable for your needs, is used correctly and protects you from STIs.

To understand how to do this it is important to have a basic understanding of the different types of infections that can be spread through sexual contact, their symptoms and consequences to health.

STIs are becoming a serious problem in the UK and figures show that their incidence continues to rise. It cannot be stressed enough that men and women are both equally responsible for helping themselves stay protected against these potentially deadly infections.

The condom

'It is important that there is a good variety of contraceptive measures available, because by providing more options, the likelihood of compliancy and people requesting and using contraception increases.'

The male condom and female condom are the only methods of contraception that can help protect against STIs, of which most can have a seriously detrimental effect on health; in some cases they can be fatal.

Designed to fit securely over the penis, the male condom is usually made from latex, but with the increasing number of latex allergy sufferers, latex free versions are also available. They come in a range of sizes ensuring a perfect fit can be found for every individual and can also be found in many colours, flavours and textures to maximise the usage and add to sexual experiences.

On the whole, condoms are considered to be very reliable, providing they are used correctly, discarded appropriately after use and are used before their expiry date. They are less effective if stored carelessly, are caught between teeth or nails, are used with non-oil-based lubricants or a spermicidal agent, or if used past their expiry date.

It is imperative that they are approved for use – look out for the European CE stamp or a British Kite Mark. This provides evidence that it has been rigorously tested for optimal reliability.

See page 20 for information on the female condom.

The Intra-Uterine Coil Device

The Intra-Uterine Coil Device (IUCD, sometimes known more simply as an IUD) is a very dependable form of contraception and involves the use of a small device being inserted into the womb with the main body remaining in the cervical canal. It can be made from plastic and/or copper and can be left in place for up to 10 years, though five years is now becoming the norm. During this time it can provide the same level of protection throughout by preventing the implantation of a fertilised egg. Fertilisation is also prevented as the copper inhibits the sperm from entering the womb.

The IUCD cannot be used by everyone and your doctor will take a full medical history and make a thorough assessment before a decision is reached. It does not protect against STIs.

Possible side effects, though not experienced by all users, may be rejection from the body (whereby it is expelled out of the womb through the vagina), irregular bleeding or risk of perforation of the womb during insertion, though this is extremely rare.

Potential benefits of selecting the coil are its longevity of use, the immediate return to normal fertility following removal of the coil and its instant affect once fitted.

At the moment there are seven main IUCDs in the UK, including the Gynefix, the Flexi-T 300 and the Multi-Safe 375.

Often included or associated with the IUCDs is the Mirena coil, which is in fact an Intra-Uterine System or IUS. This is becoming the most popular choice of inserted device as it offers almost 100% reliability, with far fewer negative side effects or risks. Also, because of its effect of lightening the blood loss during menstruation, it is often recommended as a treatment for this.

The central section of the IUCD or IUS is made from either copper or plastic and sits in the cervical canal. This stem is infused with a synthetic hormone called Levonorgestrel that works in a similar way to other synthetic forms of progesterone hormones.

The hormone implant

The contraceptive implant is a tiny match sized device that is inserted just under the surface of the skin. It slowly releases progestogen, a man-made form of the naturally occurring hormone progesterone, into the blood stream which takes effect once it has reached the reproductive organs. Like other progesterone based contraceptives, it works by thickening the cervical mucus (which helps prevent sperm from getting through) and thinning the lining of the womb (which helps to prevent a fertilised egg from implanting and developing into an embryo).

The biggest benefits include its reliability, the fact that it can provide up to three years cover (unless it is removed or rejected, which is rare) and its ability to reduce period pain. Research suggests that it may help to protect against pelvic inflammation due to the thickening of mucus which acts as a barrier to some infections.

The down side of choosing the implant is that in a small number of people it can cause periods to become very unpredictable, often heavier and more prolonged for the first year.

At the present time, Implanon is the only type of contraceptive implant available in the UK.

The hormone implant:

- Does not protect against STIs.

- Provides long term contraceptive protection.

- Is very reliable.

- Can cause irregular bleeding.

- May take a while to settle.

The hormone injection

In 1992, the Food and Drug Administration (FDA) approved the release of the most commonly used contraceptive injection, Depo-Provera. Earlier types were seen in the 1970s but these were not routinely offered to all women.

Depo-Provera and Noristerat are the only types of hormone injections used for their contraceptive qualities in the UK at the present time, though other countries can offer others.

The injections contain a hormone called progestogen which prevents pregnancy by preventing ovulation, thickening the mucus in the cervix and by thinning the inside layer of the uterine cavity.

Careful consideration should be given before receiving either of these injections as they cannot be reversed and will act as a contraceptive for up to two months if Noristerat is chosen or three months if Depo-Provera is used.

The benefits are that you only need to remember about contraception when the next injection is due, they are extremely reliable and they don't interfere with sex. It is also thought that they may provide some protection against certain cancers and pelvic inflammatory disorders and these possibilities continue to be researched.

The disadvantage of using the injection is the potential of disruption to menstrual bleeding, which may become erratic, heavier and, in a small number, almost constant. There is also a possibility of suffering from headaches and breast tenderness.

The hormone injection or implant will not give any protection against STIs and must be used with a condom to ensure sexual safety.

When the injection is discontinued, fertility is not instantly restored and it may take from between the time of the last jab to over a year to return to normal.

The hormone injection:

- Can provide longer term contraceptive cover.

- Will not prevent STIs.

- May cause disruption to the menstrual cycle.

- Does not need to be taken everyday or at every sexual experience.

Contraceptive patches

The contraceptive patch is a fairly new development. Worn by women, this is similar to a plaster in that it is adhered to the skin. It works by slowly releasing hormones (contained in the patch) into the body, which prevent pregnancy. It can be extremely beneficial to those who are sensitive to the side effects of the oral contraceptive pill as it does not enter the digestive tract, preventing many of the digestive upsets that might occur. Remembering to take a pill every day is also eliminated, making this quite an attractive option.

Although it is reliable, there is also a risk of the patch losing its ability to stay stuck to the skin, which puts it at risk of falling off or being easily rubbed off, often without the user being aware of it happening.

'The hormone injection or implant will not give any protection against STIs and must be used with a condom to ensure sexual safety.'

Unlike the pill, it cannot control bleeding and does not reduce the symptoms of problematic and painful periods.

In a few cases, it may cause a minor skin irritation due to the nature of the adherent substances used, the most common skin reactions being slight redness or localised inflammation. The severity of the reaction can vary widely between users, with some women not being worried or inconvenienced by the reaction and some finding it bad enough to not continue using the patch.

The contraceptive patch:

- Is reliable.

- Is discreet.

- May come off if skin is oily or wet.

- May cause some degree of irritation to the skin.

- Cannot control bleeding.

- May not help improve problematic periods.

- Does not protect against STIs.

The diaphragm/cap

The diaphragm was invented as a way of preventing sperm from gaining entry into the womb by being placed in the vagina. They are traditionally made from rubber, so caution must be exercised in those who think they may be sensitive to natural rubber latex.

The cervical cap included in this category is similar to the diaphragm but is much smaller and fits over the cervix.

Each diaphragm or cap must be accurately sized for each individual and all users should be shown how to fit it correctly for maximum comfort and protection.

They can be cumbersome and some users report that they can interfere with sexual practices as they have to be fitted manually and should be used in conjunction with a spermicidal agent.

They provide a fairly reliable level of protection, do not carry any side effects that other contraceptives may cause and, if used long term, they are an awful lot cheaper than other forms of contraception.

The diaphragm and cap:

- Can be used on an as-and-when basis.

- Can be designed to your individual size and shape.

- Does not entirely protect against STIs.

- Is fairly reliable.

- May take a few attempts to fit correctly.

The vaginal ring

A relatively new inclusion in contraceptive medicine, the vaginal ring is a small plastic ring that is infused with both oestrogen and progesterone. It can stay in the vaginal canal for three weeks, after which it is removed for seven days, allowing for a menstrual bleed.

It remains in place with help from the vaginal wall and muscles, and if fitted correctly it should not be uncomfortable. If you are put off by having to fit the device yourself, it is important to say that with practise this can be achieved in just a few seconds.

It does not interfere with love-making and can provide almost total effectiveness if used correctly.

The most common brand used worldwide is the NuvaRing. This is not available through the NHS as yet but can be gained from private clinics.

The vaginal ring:

- Cannot be felt.

- Is thought to be reliable.

- Is not yet commonly available on the NHS.

- Does not protect against STIs.

The female condom

The female condom, or Femidom as it is called in the UK, was introduced around 10 years ago. Similar to the male condom, it is a cylindrical shaped device that is open at one end and closed at the other. It is designed to be worn inside the vaginal canal and act as a lining preventing sperm from entering the womb.

The female condom can also help to provide protection against the transmission of sexual infections if used correctly.

Provided it is used before any contact between the penis and the vagina, or hands that have been in contact with the erect penis and vagina, it is very effective. However, care should be taken when fitting it as sperm can be present in the seminal fluid excreted by the male before ejaculation. Pregnancy can still occur if this sperm is permitted to travel inside the vagina.

Like the condom, the Femidom should be handled with care and stored responsibly. They should be discarded appropriately after use and should never be used past the expiry date.

Each packet of female condoms should carry an instruction guide detailing how to fit it correctly. These instructions should be followed exactly to ensure maximum protection.

The female condom:

- Is reliable.

- May help to protect against some STIs but not all.

- Is cheap and readily available.

- Does not need a prescription.

- You may need to practise to get it to fit properly.

Spermicides

A spermicide is a substance that has been created with the aim of 'killing' live sperm before it passes through the cervix. Spermicides should only be used alongside a reliable barrier method of contraception, such as a condom, as they are not reliable enough to use on their own.

Caution must be taken when using condoms as some varieties of spermicidal agents still contain compounds that can damage the integrity of condoms, though this is becoming rare in the UK.

As spermicides can be purchased in an assortment of different forms (such as creams, gels, foams and barrier films) and in a selection of colours and aromas, many couples enjoy using spermicides as part of their love-making. However, it should be noted that users may become sensitive to the products over time – if this happens, the spermicide should be discontinued or another variety used.

Spermicides:

- Do not protect against STIs.
- May interfere with the integrity of condoms.
- Cannot be used on their own as a contraceptive.
- May be included and enjoyed in foreplay.

Using sexual techniques

By far the least reliable method of birth control is depending on sexual techniques to provide protection. It is not recommended by healthcare professionals, unless religious beliefs prevent the use of any type of contraception being used.

This method relies on the male partner ensuring that the penis is withdrawn from the vagina before ejaculation occurs. As seminal fluid contains live sperm and can leak from the penis before ejaculation, there is still a fairly high chance of conception occurring.

This method requires the female to have total trust and belief that the man will withdraw and have some degree of control over his ejaculation, which, again, is not a reliable method – many ejaculations occur very quickly with little warning.

Using this method does not protect against STIs – so, if you don't want an unplanned pregnancy or STI, ensure you use a condom.

Using sexual techniques:

- Does not provide protection against STIs.
- Is the least reliable form of contraception.

The rhythm method

This is possibly the most complicated form of birth control. It relies on finding out scientific information such as body temperatures, ovulation and menstrual cycle so the couple can determine when the female is at her most fertile and so avoid sex.

This method is not particularly reliable and does not ensure protection against STIs.

The rhythm method:

- Is not recommended as a reliable way of providing contraceptive cover.
- Does not provide any protection against STIs.
- Needs several attempts to perfect it.

The oral contraceptive pill

Designed to be taken by women (although a male alternative is being developed), the pill is a tiny tablet that contains hormones, some natural and others man-made, which are absorbed into the body. It prevents pregnancy in a number of ways and will be described and explained throughout the remainder of this book.

To protect against STIs you will need to combine the pill with using a condom.

The contraceptive pill:

- Provides almost total contraceptive cover.
- Is used by millions of women globally.
- Does not provide protection against STIs.
- Can cause some side effects.
- Comes in many different forms.
- Can help protect against other illnesses and conditions.

Checklist

- Contraceptives are predominantly based on either hormone control or work as a barrier to sperm.
- Most contraceptives are designed to be used by females.
- A general awareness of the different types of contraception helps individuals to make an informed and educated choice regarding contraception.
- Using sexual technique or the rhythm method are the least effective forms of birth control and do not provide any protection against STIs!

'To protect against STIs you will need to combine the pill with using a condom.'

Summing Up

Any man or woman who is sexually active, but doesn't want to start a family right away or wants to find out more about protecting themselves from STIs, will benefit by learning about all the possible forms of contraception available to them; how to use them, how they work, who they are available for and where to get them. Only by being equipped with all the facts can a fully informed decision be made.

'There are many different types of contraception available that can be used by either a male or female, with some having additional benefits to health and some being deemed unsuitable.'

There are many different types of contraception available that can be used by either a male or female, with some having additional benefits to health and some being deemed unsuitable.

Each type has its own benefits and disadvantages, some can be administered by the individuals themselves, whilst others require medical intervention or a minor procedure.

Only the male condom will provide protection against STIs, so it is essential to make sure these are used with other forms of contraception to stay protected.

Chapter Three

The Contraceptive Pill

A brief history of the contraceptive pill

Most women are not really too concerned about the history or development of the contraceptive pill and it is not often particularly relevant. However, it can be helpful to know and understand your medications, to know where they came from and how they became the common medications that we use today.

What is the pill?

The pill is a method of contraception designed to be taken by women, protecting against unwanted pregnancies. It gives you better control over your reproductive cycle and can help you plan for a family more accurately.

They are very tiny tablets containing hormones which act in a number of different ways in the body, such as preventing the sperm from reaching the womb, stopping ovulation or preventing a fertilised egg from implanting into the wall of the womb.

The pills are taken orally, often requiring you to take it around the same time every day and, in some types, in the correct sequence. Some varieties require a break of seven days before starting a new pack while others involve taking the tablet every day with no break.

None of the pills available at the moment are designed to protect against any of the STIs or diseases, so you will need to combine this with another form of protection, such as the condom.

Who created the pill?

Often described as one of the most important and influential medications of the 20th century, the pill has come a long way since it was first discovered.

The female oral contraceptive pill was first created in the early 1950s by an Austrian man named Carl Djerassi in a modest laboratory found in Mexico City. It was discovered as a matter of course whilst Dr Djerassi and his team were trying to create a suitable treatment for menstrual complaints. The early forms of the drug were tested on Haitian women and contained oestrogen and progestin (the synthetic form of the hormone progesterone).

Once the effects of the hormones were documented, the findings allowed other scientists such as John Rock and Gregory Pincus to develop the idea into some of the earliest forms of contraceptive medications, including the combined oral contraceptives we know today which are based on these developments.

The first type developed was the combined pill and, once it was released for general use, it quickly became the most widely used form of contraception.

Due to some of the reported side effects of the combined pill, a progesterone-only pill, known as the mini pill was developed and released in the 1980s.

Why was it developed?

As abortion at this time was illegal and the only other methods of contraception available for general use were the diaphragm and the condom, the pill was the first option that gave women sole responsibility over their family planning. It revolutionised the lives of millions of women, allowing them the autonomy to choose the optimal time to start their family if they wished to have one, while allowing the freedom to continue to enjoy a healthy sex life.

The pill has not gone without controversy though. Many people opposed this medication, stating that it allowed people too much sexual freedom and interfered with nature's way, preventing the growth of the population and the natural occurrence of childbirth. There were arguments between many groups from feminist parties, religious groups and even within marriages.

Along with these issues, there were concerns among the medical professions who were extremely cautious of the long term effects the pill might have on health and what problems it might present for users in the future. There were also many health scares over the years, which were blamed on pill usage. Fortunately, as research continued, many of these fears were nullified and doctors became more confident at prescribing the pill to many women. The benefits far out-weighed the possible side effects, providing the users did not possess any of the medical conditions that are now known to be contraindicated with contraceptive pill usage.

When did it become available for general use?

The oral contraceptive pill first became available on the NHS in 1961. The Health Minister at the time, Enoch Powell, issued a press release but did not stipulate who the pill was designed for or whether there were any potential side effects or long term risks.

The pill is now used by well over 3 million women in the UK, most of whom are between the ages of 16 and 50, though it has been prescribed for those younger than 16 (the legal age of consensual sex). This has caused further arguments and debate among several different groups as people worry it advocates or justifies underage sex. Many doctors have come against stiff opposition, having to defend their decision to offer the pill to these girls.

Despite these conflicts of interest, the pill is now thought to be used by around 100 million women worldwide and is the form of contraception women are most familiar with.

'The pill is now thought to be used by around 100 million women worldwide and is the form of contraception women are most familiar with.'

How has it evolved?

Contraceptive devices and methods have been around since the ancient Egyptians who created very primitive forms of the condom, and they have evolved over time to the many different forms that are used by many today.

When the pill became readily available, its usage grew quickly, allowing women more autonomy over their own fertility and choices. As side effects were discovered and some women were found to be unsuitable candidates for existing types, research and various companies prompted the development of several different brands that could help women in these categories.

The mini pill was developed in the 1970s and was particularly popular with those who couldn't take oestrogen based products and those who did not find the combined pill suitable. Although this pill carries fewer side effects than the combined pill, it is slightly less effective for a variety of reasons and is not as popular as the combined pill in modern society.

Despite the pill's common usage among liberal women, there was some uncertainty about the withdrawal bleed as many women rely on the event of a period to reassure them that they aren't pregnant. When taking the pill, the bleeding that occurs during the pill free week is not actually a period at all but a result of the drop in hormones, which some women felt to be disconcerting. In spite of this, its popularity grew and it soon became the leading contraceptive.

Research continued to refine the hormonal content in the pills and dosages were gradually lowered until the very reliable forms of tablets we use today were perfected.

Continuing research is now looking into a form of oral contraception that can be taken continuously without the need for a pill free week, allowing women to be almost totally protected against unplanned pregnancy without the worry of remembering to start a new packet of pills or remembering which sequence to take them in. As there will be no 'period', this option may not be desirable for all women as many feel reassured that they are not pregnant when they have their monthly bleed, although this is not actually a true period nor a sign of a contraceptive failure.

Why choose the pill?

There are a number of different reasons why you might choose the pill as your preferred method of birth control:

- It may be that you simply see it as 'the done thing' and that it is expected of you. You are equipped with knowledge of several different contraceptives and have made an informed decision, weighing up the benefits against the negatives.

- Perhaps a family member has recommended it or the doctor suggested it.

- You feel it will help with your menstrual cycle.

- It's easily available.

- Its effects are reversible.

- It's easy to take.

- The contraceptive pill is free.

Whatever your reasons, taking the pill should be taken seriously and a commitment made to ensure that it is used as directed. Many women have found themselves pregnant even though they are on the pill, but when questioned it has become clear that they have not followed directions or have not been fully informed of all the issues surrounding their type of pill.

For some women, the myths associated with using the pill may have persuaded them not to use it; again this is something we will address.

The different types of pill

In the UK at the present time there are three commonly used types of contraceptive pill. These are the combined pill, the mini pill and the emergency contraceptive pill (the morning after pill).

Research continues to investigate birth control techniques and scientists are currently trying to determine the safety of a pill that is taken everyday (with no pill free week and therefore no withdrawal bleed).

There are over 20 brands of pill available to UK women, with manufacturers continuing to introduce new forms all the time. This large selection is due to many factors but mainly because each woman will respond individually to each type of pill, making some more suitable for them than others. It is not uncommon to find that you might suffer from side effects of one particular type of pill and if another type is tried, these effects will often be predominantly less or non-existent.

'There are currently between 20 and 30 different types of contraceptive pill available worldwide, each comprising of different levels of hormones.'

As funding in the health service is frequently stretched, this can be one way in which budgets are not exceeded. Your doctor will still choose a suitable form for your needs, so you needn't worry that your prescription is not right for you. However, it may be beneficial to do a little research before seeking a change so that you are armed with some evidence and information about the other types!

Who can prescribe the pill?

In the UK, anyone who holds a licence to prescribe is permitted to prescribe the pill. In the past, only doctors were permitted but now some nurses are able to obtain a licence and so it is not unusual for some senior practice nurses to legally and safely prescribe the pill.

Nurses who are able to prescribe the pill may be employed at a GP surgery, in Family Planning Clinics (see the Family Planning Association for contact details of your nearest clinic) or even through the Brook Advisory Centres.

In brief

- The combined pill contains both oestrogen and progesterone.
- The mini pill contains only progesterone based hormones.
- The emergency pill (morning after pill) was developed alongside the combined pill but was more widely promoted and used from the early 1990s.
- The male pill continues to be researched and scientists are hopeful for making it available for general use soon.

Summing Up

The pill was first discovered by accident in 1950s Mexico, where it was tested on local women. The findings were developed further, leading to the release of the combined pill in the 1960s. However, it was initially surrounded by fears from both the public domain and the healthcare sector.

Following reports from women that the combined pill was not suitable for them, the mini pill was created in the 1980s and offered to those who were unable to take the combined pill.

Some groups such as religious parties condemned the use of the pill as they believed it allowed women sexual freedom and the ability to time when they started a family, which in most religions was seen as God's will and not independent choice.

Research allowed scientists to discover how it affected immediate health and provided contraceptive cover, but they still were unsure of the long term effects.

Over the years, the pill has been the most researched and controversial drug on the market.

There are currently between 20 and 30 different types of contraceptive pill available worldwide, each comprising of different levels of hormones – some being natural hormones and some being synthetic.

Research continues and scientists are now developing a male contraceptive pill and one that allows women full contraceptive cover with the liberty of having fewer or even no monthly bleeds.

Chapter Four

The Pill - Myths or Facts?

Why are there so many myths?

There are many myths and rumours surrounding the pill, some true, some simply fabrication. Often women seem dissuaded from using the pill because they have been misinformed about the side effects or have been scared off by health scares and stories in the press. It is true that the pill can have some side effects for some women and that there are some risks involved as there are with any medications, but it is important for you to understand the actual facts based on scientific research and not just from what you have learned from friends, colleagues or family members, which may or may not be true.

A few women have had bad experiences, such as ill effects or unexpected occurrences, when taking the pill and often these incidences reach the headlines, appear as stories in magazines or are spread by word of mouth. Only when these figures (which are normally very small) are weighed-up against the millions of women who use the pill worldwide and experience none of these effects can the true facts about the pill be found.

Remember, when you possess all the facts, you can make an informed decision regarding birth control selection.

Does the pill cause weight gain?

This has been a subject of much argument for many years. It is difficult to blame the pill for weight gain when there is no supporting scientific evidence to confirm this myth.

Although it is generally believed that the older and stronger versions of the pill may have contributed to weight gain to some degree, there is very little evidence to suggest that modern varieties cause any weight gain or fluid retention.

Doctors agree that the progesterone contained in the pills may contribute to an increase in appetite but the actual pill itself does not cause the weight gain. Women who do put on weight when they start the pill are highly likely to have gained this weight regardless of whether they were taking the pill or not.

Similarly, those who have been taking the pill for many years have complained that their weight has slowly increased. However, doctors argue that this is a natural occurrence and would have occurred whether oral contraceptives were being taken or not.

'Doctors are a great source of information and will be able to advise you on other forms of contraception that may be suitable.'

I am under 16, will my doctor tell my parents?

Although you may be encouraged to confide in your parents or a close relative, your doctor is not legally obliged to tell any other party about your medical health; this includes using the pill. He or she must keep medical notes confidential.

Doctors are a great source of information and will be able to advise you on other forms of contraception that may be suitable. A close friend may help counsel your emotional well-being, but for the facts and questions about the pill, it is advised that a professional health worker is consulted.

Most doctors understand the sensitivity of this issue and, while they are likely to discourage you from beginning a sexual relationship, they will probably have a chat about protection from STIs.

If you are obtaining contraceptives from your school nurse, they may be forced to adhere to school policy which requires them to inform the school principle or even your parents. If you are concerned about this, always ask the nurse about the school policy before obtaining a prescription.

Does the pill make periods less painful?

The combination pill may be useful in helping to reduce period pain and doctors will often explain this advantage to you if you are thinking about using it as your chosen method of contraception. This type of pill has the advantage of reducing the thickness of the endometrial layer (the lining of the womb), which means it contains less blood – making periods less painful.

Doctors are unlikely to prescribe the pill for treating painful periods alone as there are many types of effective pain relieving medications available that do not have such strong effects on the body and are likely to be more effective. If your periods are extremely painful, you should speak to your doctor as there may be a treatable reason for the excessive pain.

The oral contraceptive pill and breast tenderness

There may be evidence to suggest that the pill may cause some mild breast discomfort in the early weeks or months after it is first used, but it should ease after continued usage and is not serious. Wearing a fully supportive bra will help to soothe any discomfort.

It is, however, important to perform regular checks on your breasts to assess any changes or lumps that may develop. If they do, an appointment should be made immediately with your GP.

Does the pill make bleeding lighter?

Many women will agree that the pill does make their bleeding lighter. This is because the lining of the womb contains less blood.

The hormones in the pill do not allow the lining to become engorged with blood as it would do in a normal cycle (this happens in preparation of the possibility of a fertilised egg implanting). Instead, it remains thin and, as a result, bleeds can often be quite a lot lighter than they were before the pill was taken.

Taking the pill continuously

Although it is possible to take two or more packets of the pill consecutively and not have a bleed, it is not recommended as common practice.

As explained earlier, the bleeding experienced with the pill is not a true period and is not the shedding of a thickened endometrial layer (the pill prevents this layer from becoming thickened in the first place). It is merely a slight drop in hormones that causes a small amount of blood in the existing lining to be excreted. Due to these reasons, most people who do take the pill on occasion without having a break will indeed find that they usually won't have a period.

All medications should be taken as directed but it is not unheard of for women to take up to three months of pills with no break and display no obvious side effects.

Every woman is different and will experience her own encounters with the pill individually. It is always advised that you consult your GP who has access to your health records and can make a recommendation individual to you.

'It is always advised that you consult your GP who has access to your health records and can make a recommendation individual to you.'

Not having a break from the pill is dangerous!

This is one of the most common misconceptions regarding contraceptive pill usage. There is no evidence to suggest that needing a break from taking the pill is a necessity.

Many women gain assurance that their 'normal' cycle is still fully functioning by taking a few months or even years break from the pill, but this is not a requirement unless you feel you want to try for a baby, choose another form of contraception or have been told to stop taking the pill by your doctor. If you feel happy to continue and there is not a reason for stopping, the pill be can relied on for contraceptive cover for up to 15 years, occasionally longer if the woman is in good health.

Missed pills at the beginning or end of a packet don't really matter!

This is a myth, so don't be fooled into thinking otherwise! Each pill in the packet contains the essential hormones needed to protect against pregnancy, whether it be at the beginning, in the middle or towards the end of the packet.

Women often mistakenly believe that as they are due to bleed when the packet is finished, these pills are not as important. In fact, this bleed is not a period, but simply a withdrawal bleed, and the levels of hormones must remain at a certain level throughout the packet.

Taking the pill consecutively for at least seven days will provide protection against ovulation (if using the combined pill), so missing a pill from the very middle of the packet is less risky, though it can still pose some risk and shouldn't be missed.

Does the pill cause ovarian cancer?

In fact, the opposite is true. Research has provided some reassuring evidence that those who take the pill are up to one third less likely to develop ovarian cancer than those who don't. This is especially important for those who have a strong family history of ovarian cancer and may be a reason for selecting the pill as their form of contraception.

It protects by suppressing the natural function of the ovaries and lessens the activity occurring within the organs. As the activity is reduced so to is the chance of cancerous cells developing.

Does the pill cause breast cancer?

This is an ongoing debate, with scientists analysing the results of many studies continuously.

Initial results do show that there may be a slight increase in the chances of developing breast cancer when using contraceptive pills containing high levels of oestrogen, particularly in those with close relatives who have had breast cancer. However, doctors are unsure whether these women may have developed the condition regardless of whether they were taking the pill or not and the results have not yet fully convinced doctors to withhold the pill from those in this category.

It is commonly thought and accepted that if there is an increased risk, this risk returns to the same level of probability that the women had before taking the pill.

Despite what doctors do or don't recommend, if you have a strong family history of breast cancer or have a history of breast problems yourself, you may want to ask either for the mini pill as a better option (as this does not contain any oestrogen) or seek an alternative form of contraception altogether.

Your doctor will be informed of any changes in guidelines and will be kept up-to-date with current research, allowing you to discuss your concerns in more detail.

Pill use and acne

Many doctors believe that the contraceptive pill will help to reduce acne as the condition seems to flare up at the same time during the monthly cycle; however, expert dermatologists recognise only one form of contraceptive pill (Dianette) as a method of reducing acne. It is unlikely that your doctor will prescribe this pill as a treatment for acne as there are many other available treatments that should be tried first.

If your GP is unable to help reduce your acne, you will probably be referred to a specialist dermatologist who will be able to assess your condition and plan an individual treatment regime using a variety of methods, such as lotions and antibiotics, or even more radical treatments like laser therapy.

Does the pill cause blood clots?

Taking the pill does not automatically mean you will develop a blood clot, but for those with a past history of blood clots, those with a strong family trait of blood clots or those who are overweight or smoke, your doctor may wish to have a more thorough discussion with you and assess your safety when taking the pill.

It may mean that you might not be offered the pill, or you will have to take a different type to the one you were expecting, but this will be explained to you by those prescribing the medication.

Pregnancy and the seven day pill free period

You will carry the same level of protection from pregnancy if the pill has been taken correctly. If you have taken it at the same time every day without fail, are not taking antibiotics or other medications that may interfere with its effectiveness, and do not have or have recently suffered from vomiting or diarrhoea (or any other issue that affects its mode of mechanism) you will still be protected.

You should remember that it is also important to remember to start the next packet in time as sperm can live for up to three days in the woman's body and may therefore still be viable after the next packet should have been started.

Summing Up

Since the pill was developed it has been surrounded by health scares and myths, some true and others not. These myths may have arisen from one person's bad experience, because of a lack of knowledge surrounding the pill or even as a way of putting people off using it. Fortunately, research has allowed doctors to either confirm or disregard many of these rumours and they are now more able than ever before to provide the facts and statistics for each type of pill.

It is true that there is some evidence that the pill may be dangerous to health in certain individuals; however, once you have had a full assessment by the person prescribing the pill, any risk factors can be identified and alternative methods of contraception discussed if you are not deemed suitable.

It is also true that there is substantial evidence to prove that using the pill actually helps protect against some forms of cancer, providing an added bonus for users.

Before requesting the pill, you should make sure you are equipped with all the necessary facts in order to make an informed decision concerning your method of birth control. It is also essential that you understand exactly how it should be taken to ensure maximum protection and know how to manage any occurrences when the pill is not used correctly.

'Since the pill was developed it has been surrounded by health scares and myths, some true and others not.'

Chapter Five

The Female Body

It's more complicated than you think!

It isn't just men who are baffled by the female body – as women, we seem equally confused about how we function, what is going on inside and what is and isn't normal.

Your body is made up of many different structures, including organs, bones, hormones and fluids, so to be able to fully understand the pill and how it works, it is important to have a basic understanding of a normal and healthy menstrual and reproductive function.

The female cycle

The female cycle is a recurring event that occurs as a result of hormonal changes in the body, triggered by chemicals released from glands and organs. These hormonal changes affect each woman differently and can cause changes that may result in emotional and physical differences at varying times in the monthly cycle.

Periods begin during puberty as the developing body prepares for adulthood and the possibility of pregnancy and childbirth. Some girls start their periods as early as nine, whereas others don't start until their late teens.

No two women will have the same experience of their cycle – if you've not yet started your periods, you will soon learn what is normal for you and what is not.

Many women are heavier on the first few days of their period, which lightens as the final days of bleeding pass, whilst other women will bleed the same amount for the whole period; either pattern is normal and you will learn which type of sanitary wear suits each day of your bleed. Most women use different products at different times of their period, with more absorbent products at the start and some being fortunate enough to require simple panty liners towards the end.

However, if you are post-menopausal and experience bleeding, do speak to your doctor as this may need investigating.

A brief outline of female hormones

In order to fully understand the chemicals and substances involved with the female body and those substances that are affected when taking the pill, it is useful to have a brief knowledge of the common female hormones.

Progesterone explained

'The female cycle is a recurring event that occurs as a result of hormonal changes in the body, triggered by chemicals released from glands and organs.'

Progesterone is an extremely important hormone in the female body and is not just associated with the reproductive system; it is essential for the general health of many of the body's functions and processes.

In the years preceding the menopause, progesterone is made by the ovaries. After the menopause it is then made by other organs and glands. Progesterone allows for the production of oestrogen by the ovaries, which occurs in the final two weeks of a natural cycle and encourages the chances of a healthy conception. When progesterone is being produced, the core temperature of the female body rises slightly and sometimes the detection of this temperature increase can help women struggling with conception to find out when they are at their most fertile.

Progesterone, or its synthetic equivalents called progestin or progestogen, is included in both the combined and mini pill. Essentially it acts as a way of fooling your body into thinking it is already pregnant, lessening the chances of ovulation occurring.

Progesterone also causes the existing mucus in and around the cervix to thicken, which prevents sperm from penetrating into the uterine cavity and finding an egg to fertilise.

Oestrogen explained

Oestrogen is the main female sex hormone and plays a very important role in the regulation and physiology of the menstrual cycle. Made in the ovaries, oestrogen is comprised of many compounds which act together giving the female her feminine characteristics which develop through puberty. These include formation and enlargement of breast tissue, widening of the pelvis and development of the buttocks, thighs and hips.

Oestrogen works together with other female hormones and dictates when the ovaries develop eggs, when they should be released and also when the lining of the womb becomes thickened (so it's ready for the arrival of a fertilised egg).

Oestrogen is included in the combined pill as it was discovered in development that it helps to prevent egg formation and growth in the follicles of the ovaries. It does this by inhibiting the release of the hormones responsible for allowing this process to happen. It also helps to regulate the cycle and lessen the chance of breakthrough bleeding (bleeding while taking the active pills, often called 'spotting').

Early forms of the contraceptive pill contained fairly high levels of this hormone but these have now been reduced as a matter of safety, and because a lower amount did not seem to affect its mode of mechanism.

Testosterone explained

Although testosterone is usually associated with being a male hormone, it is also found in women and is made in the ovaries, though to a much lesser degree than in a man. Its role in women is not fully understood but it is thought to contribute to libido and sex drive.

The menstrual cycle

The menstrual cycle is a regular series of physiological changes within the body. The cycle itself begins during puberty (normally occurring in early teens) and finishes when you are around 50 years old. Remember though, these figures are only averages and it is not unusual to find girls as young as nine have started their periods or as late as 18, with similar variations when they finish during the menopause, which can sometimes be in the mid to late thirties or as late as 60.

A cycle is determined as being the time between having one bleed and the next, and it varies between women. As previously explained, when the contraceptive pill is used, the monthly bleed experienced is not a true period as the lining of the womb is prevented from thickening and shedding. Instead, it is merely a withdrawal bleed and occurs mainly as a way of reassuring the female that she is not pregnant (also as women we expect and believe it is natural to bleed every month). Scientists developed the pill to contain this bleed purely for the psychological benefits to women.

The menstrual cycle is not just limited to having a monthly bleed; there are other indicators that can let you know where in your cycle you are:

- Breast tenderness.
- Heightened sensitivity.
- Lower abdominal aches or pains.
- Lower back ache.
- Increased irritability.

Sometimes you might also notice that your body temperature increases slightly, most commonly at night. Having a bath with essential oils or relaxing bubble bath may help ease these symptoms, along with a milky drink that will help induce sleep. Over time you will know what comforts you during these times and what irritates you.

Everyone is different

We are all unique in the way we function and manage processes, and the menstrual cycle is no different. Some women have extremely regular cycles that last for 28 days and have a five day bleed, whereas others have a 21 day cycle and bleed for up to eight or even nine days, and some even have up to a 35 day cycle. There is no one length of cycle that is more advantageous than another and the average cycle length is 28 days.

The flow of menstrual blood will also vary; some women will find they bleed more heavily for the first day or two and then have minimal bleeding and others may bleed evenly throughout. Some women pass clots and others don't; you are unique so don't worry if your friend's experience is totally different to yours.

Your actual pattern of cycle is not important – you just need to recognise what is 'normal' for you so that you can identify when something becomes irregular or uncharacteristic for you as an individual.

Am I normal?

As each woman's menstrual cycle is unique, it may be that you have always been 'regular', knowing exactly when you will bleed and for how long, which pre-menstrual symptoms affect you and to what degree, how much you bleed and which days are the heaviest. Though it is quite rare, some women even believe they know exactly when they are ovulating and releasing an egg. They report that they can feel a dull ache resonating from the ovary producing the egg or can feel the released egg leaving the ovary, likening it to a 'popping' sensation.

However, if you are unable to find this level of 'normality', this does not mean you are abnormal. Menstrual cycles vary widely and the same variations can be seen in the length of time between bleeds. It is not unusual for there to be 21 days between periods, nor is it uncommon for some women to have up to 35 bleed-free days between periods.

These figures assume that you do not bleed between cycles as this can also be common for some women, although it may be a sign of an underlying medical condition if it occurs when an otherwise regular cycle has been functioning for some time.

If you normally have a regular cycle of any length and suddenly find that you are bleeding irregularly, it is important to discuss this with your doctor who may want to carry out some tests to determine the cause.

If your cycle suddenly becomes longer, there are longer stretches of time between bleeds, you are bleeding for longer or you are bleeding after sexual intercourse, it is also important to get this checked out by your doctor in case

'There is no one length of cycle that is more advantageous than another and the average cycle length is 28 days.'

of hormonal imbalances, an unknown pregnancy or another medical condition. It may simply be that you are maturing and your hormone levels are changing naturally, so do not worry until you have spoken to your doctor.

What is ovulation?

Ovulation is the release of a mature egg from the ovary. The female body contains two ovaries and each ovary releases an egg on alternate months.

Before an egg is released, hormonal levels in the body change and a sequence of events occurs.

The process

- Within the brain is an area called the hypothalamus which releases a hormone called Gonadotrophin-Releasing Hormone (GnRH).

- GnRH sends a message to the pituitary gland (also located in the brain) to release a hormone called Follicle Stimulating Hormone (FSH).

- FSH is sent to the ovaries to tell them to start preparing eggs for release.

- As the ovaries are developing these eggs, the levels of oestrogen rise. The eggs are matured in small fluid filled compartments called follicles.

- Whichever follicle develops and matures its egg first becomes the dominant one and the one from which the egg will be released. When this occurs and the final stages of egg maturation occur there is a surge in oestrogen levels.

- This surge indicates to the pituitary gland that it needs to release a hormone called Luteinising Hormone (LH) which tells the follicle to release the egg.

- When the egg has been released it is caught by a fringe of fibrous tissue (called the fimbria) located at the end of the fallopian tube.

- Once caught, it travels down the fallopian tube for possible fertilisation by sperm.

The menstrual bleed occurs 14 days after the egg has been released. If you have a regular cycle, ovulation can be calculated and the optimal time for conception can be discovered.

What exactly is conception?

The achievement of conception has been described by many as the nearest thing to a modern day miracle. This is because in order to conceive, there are so many variables that have to occur and be timed perfectly.

At the time of the egg being released from the ovary, the inner lining of the womb (called the endometrium) becomes thicker in preparation for a pregnancy. Also at this time the cervical mucus is thinner, allowing easier access for sperm to enter the womb.

The basal body temperature is the temperature of your body at the time of first awakening. This temperature is calculated before any activity is carried out and may also be referred to as your resting temperature. During ovulation and conception, this temperature increases slightly to provide a more accommodating environment for an egg to survive and become fertilised.

After a man ejaculates, millions of sperm are released; some will leak out of the vagina whilst others will try and gain access to the womb via the cervix. The strongest and healthiest sperm will find their way to the womb and head for the entrance to the fallopian tube where it hopes to find an egg awaiting fertilisation.

When the two meet, the sperm enters the egg by releasing enzymes normally contained inside the sperm. These enzymes attach to the outside of the sperm and then adhere to the surface of the egg where they gradually 'eat' away at it until the outer shell has been penetrated.

In the week following fertilisation, the egg moves down from the fallopian tube into the womb and firmly implants itself to the thickened endometrium. As the egg develops and grows, the womb expands to accommodate the growing foetus.

'The achievement of conception has been described by many as the nearest thing to a modern day miracle. This is because in order to conceive, there are so many variables that have to occur and be timed perfectly.'

Summing Up

Every woman's cycle is unique and is dependent on the release of progesterone and oestrogen, which are the dominant female sex hormones. They work in conjunction with other hormones and dictate when an egg is to be released.

The process of an egg maturing and being released is called ovulation, whilst fertilisation refers to the process of an egg being penetrated by sperm. When this fertilised egg embeds into the lining of the womb, conception has occurred and the female is pregnant.

Each menstrual cycle is calculated as the time between one monthly bleed and the next, which can vary between women. Eggs are released exactly 14 days before the next period, allowing women with regular cycles to determine when they are at their most fertile.

Eggs are released alternately between the left and right ovaries, with the most mature of the developed eggs being the one that is released for that cycle.

Chapter Six

The Combined Pill Explained

What is the combined (or combination) pill?

By far the most frequently requested and used form of oral contraceptive, the combined pill is made up of a blend of oestrogen and progesterone – hence its title. It can come in a range of strengths, with the ratio of the two hormones being at different levels.

Thanks to research and medical development, it can now be provided with low dosages. These low dose combined pills are commonly misunderstood to be the mini pill, when in fact this isn't at all true.

How the combined-pill works

The combination of oestrogen and progesterone (known as progestin or progestogen if synthetic forms are used) aims to inhibit conception in three ways:

Prevention of an egg being released from the ovary

This is achieved by the steady release of hormones sending messages to the pituitary gland to inhibit the release of the hormone responsible for stimulating egg growth, development and release. In doing so, the sperm that reaches the womb and fallopian tube will not be able to find an egg to fertilise.

Increased cervical mucus

Mucus around the cervical canal becomes thickened thus making it more difficult for any sperm to penetrate into the womb.

Thinning of the womb lining

Without using the pill, this lining (the endometrium) usually thickens in preparation for a fertilised egg to implant. The hormones in the combined pill prevent this thickening from happening, making it impossible for an egg to embed and develop.

The different types of combination pill vary depending on the levels of hormones in the pack and the rate and timing of the release and absorption of the hormones within the body.

What are the different types of combination pill?

There are three different types of combination pill: the mono-phasic pill, the multi-phasic pill and the everyday pill.

The mono-phasic pill

The mono-phasic pill contains 21 active pills per packet with each tablet containing progesterone and a low dose of oestrogen. All the tablets contain this ratio of hormones and are released evenly into the system. As the level of hormone in the body is constant and therefore does not alter, this pill is particularly good for regulating your cycle and can be used to manipulate it. For example, if you are travelling you can take more than one packet of this pill without having the monthly withdrawal bleed; your hormone level will remain constantly the same so no bleed will occur. It is simply the withdrawal of the hormones during the pill-free week that causes a bleed.

If you want to avoid having a monthly withdrawal bleed, this practice is acceptable every once in a while – but only when completely necessary. It should not be relied upon regularly as it was not designed or intended for this type of usage.

After the 21 pills have been taken you will have a pill free week, during which you will have a withdrawal bleed. This is often lighter than your normal period.

The multi-phasic pill

The multi-phasic pill (otherwise known as the bi-phasic or tri-phasic pill) contains 21 pills per pack. Each pill contains a different level of hormone, so they must be taken in the correct sequence. This schedule is helped along by the manufacturers who colour code the pills so you can remember to take the right pill at the right time and don't mix up the doses.

Again, after the 21 pills have been taken you will have a seven day pill free stretch after which a new packet is started. During this time you will have a withdrawal bleed.

The everyday pill

The everyday pill contains 28 pills per packet – one for every day. These extra pills do not contain any hormones and exist simply to prevent the female from forgetting to re-start the pill after the seven day pill free period.

In order to ensure that the placebo pills and active pills are not taken in the wrong order, they usually come in slightly different colours. Using everyday pills does not mean you will not bleed – you will still have a withdrawal bleed.

In order to help the female use the pill correctly, manufacturers often add imprints on the packet or adhesive labels. These labels can be placed on the packet to correspond with the current day on the calendar when you first begin taking it.

However, if you are taking pills that vary in strength and dose, there is often a labelling system included that allows the user to label the first pill with whichever day of the week the pill is to be started and so on.

This may sound confusing but with a little help from your doctor, nurse or even pharmacist you will soon grasp the concept. It's just a case of getting organised!

'By far the most frequently requested and used form of oral contraceptive, the combined pill is made up of a blend of oestrogen and progesterone – hence its title.'

How effective is the combination pill?

There are many considerations when measuring the effectiveness of the pill, many of which do not necessarily concern the pill itself. This could be how many times you have sex, any other existing conditions/medications and even your age.

The biggest problem when measuring the effectiveness is trying to determine whether people are taking it correctly or not. When it is taken as directed (with no other interfering aspects) it is thought to be over 99% effective.

Aspects such as gastro-intestinal disturbances, other medications or even some complimentary therapies may interfere and lower the effectiveness of your prescription. It is advised that you always ask your doctor, pharmacist or alternative therapist for advice.

The benefits of using the combined pill

- As with using any pill, one of the biggest benefits is that sexual activity does not have to be interrupted for contraceptive purposes, such as when fitting a diaphragm. However, it is advised that a condom is used, but this can add to the sexual experience for many couples.

- As the combined pill contains both oestrogen and progesterone, the chances of maturing and releasing an egg are a lot less likely than with the mini pill.

- It is thought that the pill is good for relieving some of the discomfort or inconvenience of many of the symptoms of pre-menstrual tension. It may be offered to some women purely for this reason, although this is not very common.

- The pill has been proven to lower the chances of developing ovarian cancers and cysts, endometrial cancers, cancers of the large bowel and may protect against pelvic inflammatory disease.

- Periods often become more regular, lighter and less painful than before. There is less chance of breakthrough bleeding than there is with the mini pill.

- It is possible to take two packets together so there is no withdrawal bleed, which can be especially useful if you are going on holiday. This is safe to do once in a while, but it's not recommended to be undertaken for longer than two packets unless your doctor deems otherwise.

- The combined pill has been found to reduce the risk of benign breast diseases.

The disadvantages of using the combined pill

- The biggest disadvantage of using any type of pill is that it does not provide protection against STIs. Condoms should be worn to provide protection against STIs.

- Although it is less likely with the combination pill, there is still a small chance of breakthrough bleeding occasionally. However, this usually subsides after a few months.

- Some medications and conditions (e.g. antibiotics and diarrhoea) are likely to affect its effectiveness and other forms of contraception should be used during these times and for seven days after.

- Evidence suggests that those who suffer from migraines may find that they worsen when taking the pill.

- Some groups of people cannot take the pill (especially the combined pill) for safety reasons, for example those with a history of blood clots, those who smoke heavily, are over 35 or who are extremely overweight.

- There is a chance of suffering from headaches, nausea and breast tenderness in the first few months.

'There are three different types of combination pill: the mono-phasic pill, the multi-phasic pill and the everyday pill.'

How to take the combined pill

The combination pill should optimally be taken on the first day of your next period, although it can be delayed until the fourth day if needed. The combination pill should provide almost immediate protection against pregnancy if it is used in this way, but if it is started on day five of your period or later, it will take up to seven days to provide full cover and other forms of contraception will be needed until then.

You should take it the same time each day, i.e. on the same hour, every 24 hours, and should try and choose a time that you know you will be able to do this. Most people take it first thing in the morning, although some choose lunchtime as their best time, allowing for weekend or holiday lay-ins and so on. It really doesn't matter what time of day you start your pill as long as you can take it at the same or very similar time each day.

A lot of women have found that if they take their first pill on a Sunday, their future withdrawal bleeds will happen during the week, leaving them free to enjoy the weekends without the worry of bleeding.

Most pill packets come with some kind of labelling system such as days of the week. If this is so, always start your packet on the corresponding day. Continue to take the whole packet and then have a pill free week if you have only 21 pills in your pack, or take the final seven pills as normal everyday.

The pills can be taken with water or other fluids (obviously alcohol is not recommended) and can also be taken before or after food.

What to do if you miss a pill

Unfortunately this is quite a common occurrence – even in those who are usually very good at taking it correctly. Travelling long distances, late nights or other reasons may mean that a pill is taken very late or not at all. It is important to carry out the instructions for your prescription. Some women mistakenly believe that they will not be affected by missing pills and for many this is true, but an unwanted pregnancy is a high price to pay for not spending a few minutes reading the instructions and carrying them out.

Your action plan

The first thing to remember is not to panic. The chances of conceiving will be greatly reduced if you follow a few simple rules:

- If you have missed one pill – take it as soon as you remember and continue as normal, even if this means taking two pills in the same day or even at the same time.

Need2Know

- If you have missed two pills – take the last pill you missed then carry on taking the pills as normal. If you have less than seven days of pills left in your pack you should carry on straight into your next pack without having a pill free week.

- It should be noted that the rules may vary between each type of pill and even between manufacturers, so you should always refer to the patient information sheet included in the packet.

- If you have any concerns at all, ring your GP or the NHS Direct helpline who will be able to advise you on the correct schedule concerning your prescription.

- Consideration should also be given to whether you have been sick less than four hours after taking a pill. It may not have been absorbed by the stomach and therefore will have been ejected in the vomit. This can be classed as a missed pill.

Ensuring the effectiveness of the combination pill

The best way of ensuring effectiveness of the combination pill is to remember to take it. Taking it at the same or similar time every day is very important. Try putting it next to your toothbrush or make-up, set an alarm on your mobile phone, put it next to your glasses or contact lenses or associate it with some other daily activity that will prompt you into remembering to take it.

If you are struggling to take it or you are regularly missing pills, especially when starting a new packet, it may be worth discussing the option of using an everyday pill or another form of contraception altogether.

It is also important to understand that some circumstances and medications may affect the effectiveness of the pill. If you are suffering from vomiting or diarrhoea, you may not be protected against pregnancy as the pill may be ejected in vomit before absorption or may not be absorbed fully if you have diarrhoea. During these episodes you must make sure you use other contraception for seven days, such as condoms, or abstain from sex until you feel better and for the seven days following.

'The effectiveness of the pill is largely dependent on you taking it correctly and understanding what circumstances might interfere with its absorbency or mechanism.'

There are many medications that can interfere with the pill and these include antibiotics, anti-fungal preparations, drugs used for treating epilepsy, sleeping tablets, tranquillisers and those given for gastric problems. Always make sure you ask your doctor or pharmacist if your other prescriptions affect the pill and take other precautions as directed.

If you are taking the sort of pill that does not contain the same amount of hormone in each tablet or must be taken over 28 days, always make sure you follow the colour coding on the packet or label the pack as directed. Your doctor or pharmacist will be able to help you with this so you get the hang of it.

Checklist

- Do I have a basic understanding of the different types of this form of contraceptive pill?

- Do I know what to do if I miss a pill?

- Have I kept the enclosed patient information leaflet?

- Do I understand when to start taking the pill?

Summing Up

The combination pill comes in either 21 or 28 day packets, each containing a different level of hormones that work in slightly different ways. These hormones may be derived naturally or be man-made.

The effectiveness of the pill is largely dependent on you taking it correctly and understanding what circumstances might interfere with its absorbency or mechanism.

If a pill is missed there are certain rules to follow but these can vary between different prescriptions. The information given with each packet should always be referred to, or another source contacted if these instructions aren't clear or understood correctly.

'It should be noted that the rules may vary between each type of pill and even between manufacturers, so you should always refer to the patient information sheet included in the packet.'

Chapter Seven

The Mini Pill/Progesterone Only Pill (POP)

What is the mini pill?

Often misunderstood, the mini pill isn't simply a weaker version of the combined pill nor is it a less reliable form of the pill. Otherwise known as the progesterone only pill (POP), it is very different to the combined pill and is not used as frequently.

This form of contraception contains no oestrogen, but solely a synthetic substance called progestogen or progestin, which acts almost identically to the naturally occurring hormone called progesterone.

Like other forms of the pill, the POP is a small tablet that comes in monthly packets and should be taken daily.

How the mini pill works

These progestogen pills work differently to the combined pill as they have less effect on preventing ovulation (though this may still occur) but cause other changes in the body that help to prevent conception. The main way in which it works is by significantly thickening the mucus at the entrance and through the channel of the cervix. This prevents the sperm from being able to penetrate through to the inside of the womb where it might find an egg.

To a small degree it can also help thin the lining of the womb, making it more difficult for an egg to attach itself to the womb.

Newer versions of the mini pill are being developed and perfected, allowing them to have more of an effect on ovulation, making it increasingly reliable.

Who is it prescribed to?

The mini pill is often prescribed to women who have recently had a baby and plan to breastfeed. The combined pill can affect lactation and interfere with successful breastfeeding, whereas the mini pill can be taken without any such effects. There is also evidence that some of the hormones contained in the combined pill may be passed through the breast milk into the nursing child, which does not occur when using the mini pill.

The mini pill is also more commonly prescribed to those who have a history of high blood pressure (especially whilst taking the combined pill), those who smoke heavily and older ladies.

The disadvantages of taking the mini pill are that it is marginally less effective and it must be taken every day – thus bleeding cannot be controlled.

What are the different types of mini pill?

They are all oestrogen free and contain either progestogen or progestin as their active ingredient.

Most of the mini pills on the market are very similar and vary only between manufacturers; however there is one variety that stands out from the rest and this is called Cerazette. A fairly new and popular addition, Cerazette has been developed to encourage the inhibition of ovulation, making it even more reliable than before.

How effective is the mini pill?

The effectiveness of the mini pill is a subject of much debate. Some experts believe it is more reliable than the combination pill if taken exactly as directed, especially with the introduction of Cerazette, whilst other experts state that it is very slightly less reliable than the combination pill.

'Newer versions of the mini pill are being developed and perfected, allowing them to have more of an effect on ovulation, making it increasingly reliable.'

Overall, the effectiveness of the mini pill is generally believed to be slightly lower than that of the combined pill. While the protection is still very high if used correctly, the chances of a user error occurring are quite high and most varieties do not prevent ovulation.

Due to these reasons, the mini pill provides 90-99% protection if used as directed, though with new pills being researched and introduced all the time, this is thought to increase in the future.

The benefits of using the mini pill

- There are many benefits to using the min-pill instead of the combined pill, the biggest advantage being that it can be used by those who cannot take products containing oestrogen.

- It can be used by those who are breastfeeding.

- It is prescribed more frequently for those who are over 35.

- It is used for those who smoke moderately.

- The mini pill may be found to be more suitable in those who couldn't get along with the combined pill.

- Evidence has suggested that if used 100% correctly (though this is problematic for many users) it provides better cover against pregnancy than the combined pill. However, some figures suggest otherwise, which is evidence that its failure rate is almost purely down to user errors, though this is difficult to quantify. This highlights the need for women choosing the mini pill to fully understand how to take it properly. Some women find it intimidating when talking to their doctor about their periods but it really is essential that any questions are addressed. As a user of the mini pill, please make sure that you take the opportunity to ask any questions and are confident in how to take this form of the pill.

- It can be used by those who are overweight but not by those who are obese as the effectiveness is reduced.

- In general, it tends to cause fewer side effects than the combination pill.

- The mini pill can be useful for older women who are experiencing the first signs of the menopause and may help relieve symptoms until you can see your doctor.

The disadvantages of using the mini pill

- The mini pill does not provide protection against STIs.

- It is not suitable for everyone, including those who are severely overweight, have a history of breast cancer or have had an ectopic pregnancy (where the developing foetus grows in the fallopian tube instead of the womb).

- There is no scope for flexibility of timing or missing pills as they must be taken every day at exactly the same time.

- The mini pill does take immediate effect if taken on the first day of your period, but otherwise may take up to one month before it reaches its optimal level of protection.

- Monthly bleeding is likely to become more irregular, with the chance of additional spotting or breakthrough bleeding. However, this occurrence should settle over time, becoming less problematic for the user.

- It is possible to suffer from headaches and nausea during the first few months of taking the mini pill.

- It is less suitable for those who work erratic shift patterns as it must be taken at the same time every day.

- There is an increased chance that those on the mini pill are more likely to develop ovarian cysts, although this increase is small.

- Women who are bad time keepers or think they will have difficulty remembering to take it at exactly the same time every day will increase their risk of pregnancy significantly.

How and when to take the mini pill

Unlike the combined pill, the mini pill can be started whenever you choose. The only consideration should be at what time of the day you take your first pill. It cannot be stressed enough that it must be taken at exactly the same time every day – delaying this time by even three or four hours can reduce your level of protection enough to fall pregnant.

You should take your lifestyle into consideration when choosing which time of day to take the pill. If you have an active social life and enjoy going out regularly, picking a time when you are likely to be out is not going to be a very good idea. If these social events mean you are likely to be out of bed late in the mornings then first thing in the morning is not a good plan either. For many, the stroke of noon or before the evening meal may be more suitable.

Mini pills come in packets containing 28 pills. One should be taken every day and the next packet started immediately. You will have a bleed every month and the pills should be continued regardless of whether you are still bleeding or not. This bleed will normally happen during the last week of the packet.

What to do if you miss a pill

Missing a mini pill altogether is more serious than if a combined pill is missed because contraceptive cover is not provided for as long.

When a pill is completely missed or is taken more than four hours late, it is essential that an alternative method of contraception is used for at least one month (ideally three months). This can be either a condom, possibly combined with a spermicide (though not spermicide alone), or abstaining from sexual practices altogether.

If you have missed a pill, take it as soon as you remember and seek advice if this is over four hours later than your usual time. This may mean you take two pills in one day, which is not harmful. However, it may be harmful to take more than two pills in 24 hours so please do not do this unless you have spoken to a medical professional. Always refer to the patient information leaflet included in the packet as there will be guidelines that are appropriate to your individual prescription.

If you have missed more than two pills it is possible that you are not protected. Your doctor may advise that you use the emergency contraceptive pill if you have had sexual intercourse in the last 48 hours.

Do not assume that all is lost if you miss a pill – continue taking the remainder of the packet as directed and phone your GP or NHS Direct if you would like further advice or reassurance. See help list for NHS contact details.

Ensuring the effectiveness of the mini pill

As timing is the most important factor when taking the mini pill, it may be useful to set yourself a reminder alarm on either a watch or mobile phone to help ensure effectiveness.

It is also important to remember that certain medications, alternative therapies or sickness and diarrhoea can affect the pill. Alternative measures should be used during these times and for at least one month after.

Your pill packet will usually be labelled with the days of the week or something similar, so always remember to take whichever pill falls on the corresponding day – it makes life easier for you! If at any time you realise you are not taking the corresponding day, this can indicate that you may have forgotten to take a pill and other contraceptive methods should be used.

As many women find it takes some time to get used to taking a pill every day at the same time, it may be worth using a back-up form of contraception for a while until you have fully formed the habit.

A great method is to incorporate the use of condoms into your love-making as this not only provides protection from pregnancy, but will give good protection against STIs. It is important that oral sexual practices are performed carefully as damage from teeth, tongue piercings or even earrings can compromise the condom and may cause it to fail.

Checklist

- Do I understand how the mini pill differs from the combined pill?

- Do I understand how the mini pill prevents pregnancy?

- Do I know what to do if I miss a pill?

- Have I retained and read the patient information leaflet contained in the packaging?

Summing Up

The mini pill can be called the POP and does not contain any oestrogen.

It works slightly differently to the combined pill, although the newest forms of the mini pill have been designed to act in a very similar way.

The tablet is made from synthetic forms of the hormone progesterone and will provide adequate protection against pregnancy if taken correctly.

User error is a highly significant aspect when referring to failure rates. Unlike the combination pill, the mini pill is always taken for 28 days and the next packet started straightaway. It is essential that the tablets are taken at exactly the same time each day or within a three hour time slot.

'Missing a mini pill altogether is more serious than if a combined pill is missed because contraceptive cover is not provided for as long.'

Chapter Eight

The Emergency Contraceptive Pill

Sometimes there are circumstances in which an emergency contraceptive will be needed. Anyone who has had sexual intercourse in the last 72 hours and thinks they might be at risk of an unwanted pregnancy may want to consider seeking advice about this form of emergency contraception (also known as the morning after pill).

What is the morning after pill?

The morning after pill is a form of hormone based contraception that can be taken in any of the following eventualities:

- You have missed more than one pill and have had sexual intercourse during this time.

- Other methods of contraception have failed, e.g. the condom has broken.

- In the case of rape or sexual assault when conception may be possible.

- You have had sexual intercourse and used no protection.

It contains a high dose of progesterone, a hormone which is already produced in the ovaries, and can be taken safely by most women, including those who are breastfeeding or those who cannot take oestrogen based products.

However, it should not be used regularly; it's not as effective as other forms of contraception and most doctors will advise you on other means of contraception if you are taking this form of tablet regularly.

How does it work?

Emergency oral contraceptives have been developed a lot in recent years and differ slightly from the old varieties. Now all that is needed is a single dose that should be taken within 72 hours of having unprotected sex.

It works in three ways; by preventing ovulation if ovulation in your cycle has not yet happened, delaying ovulation if it is about to occur and preventing implantation of a fertilised egg if conception has occurred.

Many women have shown concern about whether the emergency pill actually causes an abortion to occur. Doctors distinctly agree that this is not true as an abortion can only occur after a fertilised egg has already implanted into the lining of the womb. This will not and cannot have happened using this form of contraception.

As it affects your cycle, you may find that your normal cycle is thrown slightly out of its normal pattern and your next bleed might by slightly earlier or later than normal. Don't worry about this – it occurs because of the changes in hormonal levels and will settle back down the following month.

If you miss your period totally, you should consider performing a pregnancy test as it may mean that the pill has not been successful for you. You should also seek medical advice if you experience any pain in your lower abdomen as this may indicate an ectopic pregnancy. This can be life threatening and will need urgent assessment.

Where can you get the emergency contraceptive pill?

The emergency oral contraceptive is available by prescription from your GP or Family Planning Association. It can also be purchased from a pharmacy or a private clinic for around £26 (prices subject to change), provided you are 16 years or over. Very rarely, it may be sought from a hospital accident and emergency department (but expect to wait as this is not a priority for staff), some Genitourinary Medicine (GUM) Clinics and from Brook Advisory Centres.

For those who are not yet 16, you are advised to see your GP. They will help you decide if a regular form of contraception is suitable for your needs, will talk to you about protection from STIs and will be able to access your medical notes easily.

It may be possible to obtain the emergency pill and condoms from your school nurse. However, depending on the school policy, they may be obliged to inform the school or even your parents/carers.

If you request the morning after pill, you may also want to think about whether you are at risk of an STI. Your doctor can arrange the appropriate tests for you confidentially.

If you are already taking various forms of medication, have been informed that you cannot use the 'normal' contraceptive pill or are finding that you are using the emergency contraceptive pill regularly, you must see your GP. They can advise you on other options available, prescribe the most appropriate emergency contraception and also discuss your long term contraceptive needs. Wherever you decide to obtain this pill from, compassion, confidentiality and discretion will be guaranteed.

If you have not been using contraception but have had even just one sexual partner, you will find it useful to speak to someone about the possibility of having an STI and whether you should be tested. Years ago there were a lot of negative stigmas associated with being tested for these diseases but nowadays these opinions are becoming less common and it is deemed something that people should be able to do without worry, especially if they think they might be at risk.

How to take it

In order for the morning after pill to be effective, there are certain rules that must be adhered to:

- It must be sought within 72 hours of having unprotected sex.

- The sooner after sex it is taken, the more reliable and effective it is.

- It is not to be relied on as a regular form of contraception as it is less reliable than other types and causes disruption to your normal cycle.

'Anyone who has had sexual intercourse in the last 72 hours and thinks they might be at risk of an unwanted pregnancy may want to consider seeking advice about emergency contraception.'

- You must tell the person prescribing the tablet of any existing medications or medical conditions.

How effective is the morning after pill?

The effectiveness of this tablet depends upon the length of time between having unprotected sex and actually taking the tablet. If it is taken within 24 hours, it is around 95% effective at preventing pregnancy and as time passes these rates lower slightly.

If it is taken within 24 and 48 hours, the effectiveness reduces to just over 70%. However, if it is taken after 48 hours but before 72 hours have lapsed, it provides around 50% protection.

For those who seek this tablet after 72 hours have passed, the protection rate is significantly lower and you are advised to discuss other options with your GP.

Are there any side effects?

Unfortunately, there are some side effects that may be experienced. Some women may find that they experience nausea or vomiting shortly after taking the tablet. If you have vomited, the pill may not yet have had adequate chance to absorb into the body, so protection may not be optimal and a secondary dose should be sought to provide maximum protection. This is especially true if you have vomited within two hours of taking the pill as the chances of it being absorbed are quite low.

In the event of any nausea or vomiting you should take small amounts of water frequently and eat little and often until the episode has passed.

As with other forms of hormone based medications, there may be chance of breast tenderness and the possibility of irregular bleeding but this is not serious and will subside once the tablet has been processed by the body.

Summing Up

The morning after pill can be used as a form of preventing a pregnancy if you have had unprotected sex or your regular contraception has failed.

It is most effective when taken as soon after sex as possible and becomes less reliable as time passes; it is not effective after 72 hours have lapsed.

It shouldn't be relied on as a regular form of contraception because it doesn't provide as high a level of protection against pregnancy as most other forms.

The emergency pill does not provide protection against STIs – you will need to speak to your doctor if you are concerned about this.

'If you request the morning after pill, you may also want to think about whether you are at risk of a sexually transmitted infection.'

Chapter Nine

Religious and Ethical Issues

There are many concerns among modern women surrounding the use of contraception and many of these anxieties lay not only with the implications to health, but also the effect the contraception may have within their beliefs and backgrounds and also as to how others view them.

Young teenagers who take the pill are often thought of in a negative way by others when, in actual fact, quite the opposite may be true. Their GP may have recommended the use of the pill to them or they are being very sensible and responsible.

For some, this decision should be applauded but for others there is no rationale for using the pill at a young age. There is no right or wrong answer to this subject and the only laws that stand are those that forbid sexual intercourse in those under 16.

It is a fact that in modern Britain girls are frequently having sex at a younger age and that they are more promiscuous than ever before. It is also a fact that they are now more at risk than ever of contracting an STI and, despite the many advantages of using the pill, the use of condoms should be advocated for all.

Any woman or young teenager who is sexually active has a responsibility to themselves and their sexual partners to get protection from unwanted pregnancies and STI transmission. Old fashioned judgements are not practical in today's society and fortunately most people – both old and young – are realising this.

'Any woman or young teenager who is sexually active has a responsibility to themselves and their sexual partners to protect themselves from unwanted pregnancies and STI transmission.'

Religious issues

The topic of contraception remains a controversial issue even in modern times. There are still many religious groups who condemn the use of any form of contraception and regard it as a sin.

It would be wrong to advise anyone to go against their religious beliefs, but it would also be wrong to not offer information and take choices away. If you are considering your options regarding family planning it is important to understand the facts relating to both sides of the debate.

If you have a strong religious preference you must be aware of what the ideals, recommendations and guidelines are surrounding your particular religion and belief system. This way you will know what behaviours and actions are permitted and what is forbidden.

Of course, it is not solely the purpose of family planning that contraception has been created for. More than ever it is a need to protect yourself from STIs.

Many religious groups will suggest that the only way to protect yourself is to refrain from sexual relations until you are married and safe in the knowledge that you are both free of any infections or diseases. This is indeed a sensible method of ensuring optimal safety. However, it would be foolish to believe that everyone will live by these guidelines, so provision and allowances can sometimes be permitted in these circumstances and the use of condoms advocated.

'If you have any concerns at all about how your particular religious denomination stands on the issue of contraception, why not arrange an informal chat with your religious leader and seek guidance from them?'

If you have any concerns at all about how your particular religious denomination stands on the issue of contraception, why not arrange an informal chat with your religious leader and seek guidance from them?

If you have made the decision to use a contraceptive device and are worried about how your doctor will react, you can be comfortable in the knowledge that any information regarding your health must legally remain confidential. You can also seek advice and prescriptions from other sources, for example the Family Planning Association. Of course, it is entirely recommended that you do inform your GP surgery of any medications you are currently taking as these should be included in your medical notes for future reference or in case of any complications.

Christianity

Although the Bible is quite vague and non-explicit in its opinions about contraception, experts and religious leaders have drawn views from various scriptures regarding marriage and relationships in general. Initially the church did not advocate the use of any contraception, but, with the rise in STIs, the incidence of single parents, unplanned pregnancies and termination of pregnancy, views have been modernised and contraception is now increasingly accepted when used within a marriage for family planning purposes only. It does not advocate that all girls should be able to 'go on the pill' and that people can now be promiscuous, but that it may have a place when used sensibly and in a loving and solid relationship.

However, the Catholic Church is an exception to these guidelines and it remains firm that artificial forms of contraception are not acceptable and, unless a child is planned, sexual intercourse should only occur when a woman is experiencing the most infertile part of her monthly cycle.

Islam

Like Christians who consult the Bible, Muslims who follow Islam turn to the Qur'an for guidance. Early teaching of the religion seems to advocate the rhythm method or withdrawal method as an adequate means of contraception as children are gifts from God and are given as a blessing regardless of intervention.

However, modern Muslims realise the consequences of these actions and do allow the use of contraceptives as long as fertility is not permanently affected or prevented. Islam does not encourage promiscuity and advises that contraception, indeed sexual practice as a whole, is only permitted in a loving relationship where two people are committed.

Hinduism

Within the religion of Hinduism, contraception is a subject that has been given a lot of thought and consideration. In general, the religion is very open with regard to this subject.

Those high up in the religious groups are well educated on the topic of contraception and the consequences to humanity if there are no precautions. They advise that contraception is permitted if used responsibly within a relationship. They actively encourage education on the subject, therefore allowing people the option of making informed decisions about the prevention or planning of a family.

Sikhism

Like Hinduism, Sikhism is very open to contraception and takes a modern and realistic approach to birth control and population management.

In most cases, it is for the individual couple to decide which approach they prefer and they are free to learn about and use the available types of contraception.

Judaism

Judaism is a more complicated religion and has mixed views on the subject of contraception.

Orthodox Jews believe that there is a duty to marry and have a family, that the passage of semen should be unobstructed and that any means of preventing the semen from fulfilling its purpose should be forbidden. Due to this, the use of condoms or other male birth control methods are not allowed.

More modern forms of Judaism understand the need for contraception and allow it within a relationship in order to extend the space between children, to protect the health of the mother and to prevent a family from being too high in numbers. However, it shouldn't be used to prevent children permanently or finitely. This permission has been granted after interpretation of ancient scriptures that can be applied to the modern world and modern conveniences. As a whole, this faith is very adaptable and allows a loving and committed couple to plan their family sensibly.

Buddhism

This faith is quite definite in its beliefs regarding contraception. Contraceptive measures are permitted as long as they do not interfere with a fertilised egg or kill any developing life. It can be taken from this that contraceptive devices such as the pill are permissible as they prevent conception, but that other methods such as the Intra-Uterine Device or coil are not recommended as they may destroy an egg that has been fertilised.

Buddhists agree that sexual activity should only be pursued by those in a couple wanting to pro-create; sexual encounters should not take place purely for pleasure and the use of contraception for this cause is not acceptable.

Jehovah's Witnesses

Jehovah's witnesses follow the belief that life is sacred and everyone should practice a sober life. They are relatively open about contraception and allow it as a preventative to conception, but, similarly to Buddhists, they do not permit the use of devices or methods that may inhibit the development of a fertilised egg.

Ethical issues

Ethical issues are not restricted to those with deep religious or moral opinions as anyone can find some practices ethical or indeed unethical. There are many ethical issues surrounding the use of the contraceptive pill and these may arise for either the user or the provider.

Your doctor has an obligation to protect and maintain your welfare at the same time as taking into account your wishes and beliefs. They should not allow their own personal beliefs to interfere with your autonomy and rights.

By providing you with all the facts and explaining all the advantages and disadvantages, your doctor can be sure that you are making an informed decision. Only this method of patient care can ensure that the ethics of contraception use are acknowledged.

'If you have a strong religious preference you must be aware of what the ideals, recommendations and guidelines are surrounding your particular religion and belief system.'

However, doctors are not permitted to enforce their own beliefs onto their patients and should not advocate one form of contraception over another. Nevertheless, they do have an obligation to protect their patients from harm so are within their rights to discuss the use of condoms for STI prevention.

If your doctor is of the religious belief that contraception is something that they would not use, they cannot expect their patients to have the same beliefs and should respect your own individual decisions as long as you understand the facts and implications.

Unfortunately, we live in a world full of infections that are spreading very quickly and in order to protect the population and to prevent children being born when they are not wanted, perhaps the doctors have an obligation to at least explain contraception to their patients. On the other side of the argument, there are claims that doctors should not provide information unless it is asked for; that way they cannot be accused of influencing or pressurising patients into making decisions they do not want or are not ready for.

For the most part, doctors will be able to tell from your questions and body language what your level of comprehension on the subject is. If you have any questions, please do ask them or phone one of the many help lines available to the public.

Summing Up

It is not purely health reasons that may influence a person's birth control choice. Ethical dilemmas and religious considerations also play a major role for many people.

Whatever your religious preferences and beliefs, there is no harm in finding out as much information as possible and having a chat with someone you can trust and who is in possession of all the facts.

A lot of religions are modernising their beliefs and advice about contraception – especially as today's world has a surging population with high incidences of unplanned and unwanted pregnancies outside of wedlock or committed relationships. This has forced senior religious leaders to re-evaluate their beliefs and adapt interpretations from ancient scriptures to fit in with our changing world.

Many of the older attitudes to contraception are also changing and reflect the needs of a modern woman. That said, there is no reason for any woman to feel obliged to take contraceptive measures. You have the freedom as an autonomous female to make these choices yourself or as part of a couple.

'Your doctor has an obligation to protect and maintain your welfare at the same time as taking into account your wishes and beliefs.'

Chapter Ten

The Law

Legal issues and your doctor

Many young girls report that they are afraid to speak to their doctor either because they are embarrassed or because they fear that the doctor will pass the information to a family member.

However, there are many legal obligations that doctors must adhere to in order to continue practicing medicine. Doctors must keep all information confidential and will be in breech of their Hippocratic Oath if they disclose information about their patients. They can also lose their job.

Consent

When you decide the pill might be beneficial to you, whether for contraceptive purposes or because of problematic periods, you can be certain that you will be seen by a doctor or other qualified healthcare professional and your request will be taken into consideration. There are no legal age limits for obtaining the pill and each person will be assessed as an individual.

Even if you are under 16 (the legal age of consensual sex in the UK), you can still ask for the pill and consent is not legally required from a parent or guardian.

You will, however, need to show that you are mature enough to take the pill correctly and you will usually be advised on the use of condoms and the advantages of being honest with your parents/carers.

'There are no legal age limits for obtaining the pill and each person will be assessed as an individual.'

Confidentiality

As mentioned earlier, doctors (and nursing staff) have a professional obligation to keep all information about their patients confidential. They are not permitted to disclose anything contained in patients' records into the general public domain. If they are found to have done this, they will suffer serious consequences as they have to uphold requirements written in professional codes of practice.

Any subjects that are discussed during a conversation with your doctor or those who work with your doctor, including secretaries and receptionists, are to be treated with the same level of confidentiality as medical history and prescriptions.

Some people feel they are unable to go to their usual doctor to obtain the pill as often this doctor has known the family for several years and may have a good relationship with family and friends. However, they are not allowed to disclose any information and you will be treated with the same level of respect and confidentiality as you would be by other doctors.

Although you may feel uncomfortable about asking your usual GP for the pill, it may be beneficial as the information can be documented on your health records. This can be useful for doctors in the future when looking at past medical history as they will have the full records. However, this is just a recommendation and not a requirement – take whatever action you feel most comfortable with.

Your doctor may recommend that you talk honestly to your family about your health – this is purely a suggestion and does not mean they will discuss your appointment with your parents, family or school.

When you make an appointment to see a doctor about getting the pill, he or she is not automatically obliged to give you the prescription. You will need to demonstrate that you are mature enough to understand how it works and how to take it correctly. Only after talking to you for some time about the medication will the doctor make the decision to give the pill. Making the appointment and being sensible enough to understand your need for the pill in the first place shows a sign of maturity which will be taken into account.

'When you make an appointment to see a doctor about getting the pill, he or she is not automatically obliged to give you the prescription. You will need to demonstrate that you are mature enough to understand how it works and how to take it correctly.'

It may be beneficial to tell your school nurse (if you have one) that you have decided to use the pill. In the event of a medical emergency, he or she will be able to inform the medical professionals of your existing medications more quickly than if they have to wait for your medical records to be accessed. Please be aware, however, that the only exception to the confidentiality rules concern school nurses; depending on the individual school policy, they may be contractually obliged to inform the school and/or parents/carers of contraceptive choice. It may be worth checking with the school nurse about their obligations if this is a concern. In general though, nursing staff are also obliged to maintain confidentiality.

Your individual responsibilities

Once you have made the step to ask for the pill, you will need to offer the commitment needed to ensure it is successful. This includes being able to take it efficiently each day and remembering to obtain a repeat prescription. There is little point in getting the pill if you fail to take it correctly and find yourself in the difficult situation of an unexpected pregnancy.

Your doctor will talk you through how to take the pill effectively and will want you to demonstrate that you understand how it should be taken, when to take it, when to obtain the next prescription and what situations may affect its effectiveness and how to avoid them.

If you are severely overweight it may be that you are asked to lose some excess weight before the pill is granted. Doctors have an obligation to protect your health if it is thought that the pill may do more harm than good. This does not mean the pill is unsuitable for you or that you will not get it in the future, but that at the current time it is in your best interests to seek an alternative form of contraception until you can take the pill more safely.

This is also true of those who smoke heavily as the risks associated with the pill are increased significantly and it may not be advantageous to your health to take the pill. In these circumstances your doctor will help you find a suitable alternative that can be used instead.

'Your doctor will talk you through how to take the pill effectively and will want you to demonstrate that you understand how it should be taken, when to take it, when to obtain the next prescription and what situations may affect its effectiveness and how to avoid them.'

Disclosing medical history and existing complaints

It cannot be stressed enough that any existing medical conditions should be disclosed to your doctor or the person who is prescribing the pill for you. It is in everyone's best interests to alert the doctor of any possible lifestyle issues, illnesses or experiences that may interfere with the pill and may save your life in the long run.

Conditions that may seriously affect whether the pill is safe for you to use include:

- Any history of blood clots, heart problems or stroke.

- The amount you smoke.

- Whether there is a history of high blood pressure.

- If there is any history of breast cancer, either personally or in your immediate family.

If you have experienced any of these conditions it does not automatically mean that you will not be given the pill, but the doctor can make a suitable assessment of your individual needs and can suggest the most appropriate form of pill.

The best advice is to speak honestly with the doctor as this will achieve the best result for your own individual circumstances. Medical staff have seen all sorts of people with many conditions and will not be shocked by anything you have to say. They are there to help you and can only achieve this if they are in possession of all the facts. You will not be judged in any way.

If you are nervous about asking for the pill, you may find it easier to take a close friend to your appointment. They will help you relax and after the appointment will be able to help you remember all the information that was given. You might also find it easier to talk to a female doctor instead of a male; this is a reasonable request and can be arranged by asking the receptionist specifically for an appointment with a female doctor.

Summing Up

As medical professionals, doctors and nurses have a legal obligation to keep all patient information confidential and this includes any subjects discussed during a consultation. Medical secretaries and receptionists are also legally obliged to keep all patient information confidential and legally have no right to ask why you want to see a doctor. So, there is no need to worry about asking your doctor for the pill – you will not be judged!

As a patient, it is recommended that you be as honest as you can regarding medical history. Try and disclose as much relevant information as possible in order for the doctor to assess your individual circumstances and make the best selection of contraception for you.

In order to obtain the pill you will be required to show that you are mature enough to take it correctly and understand the basic information needed to ensure it is most effective.

'As medical professionals, doctors and nurses have a legal obligation to keep all patient information confidential and this includes any subjects discussed during a consultation.'

Chapter Eleven

Common Questions

Before going to see a healthcare professional about obtaining the pill, it is worth spending some time thinking about any questions you may have. This is especially important if you have any existing medical complaints that you think might be affected by the contraceptive or any other issues that are individual to you.

It may be that you want to ask about repeat prescriptions, how to identify any physical emergencies relating to the pill or even something like how to make sure the packet is labelled clearly if you have to do this yourself. Whatever your concerns, it is always best to ask someone who is qualified to answer them rather than risk being misinformed by someone who has little knowledge of the subject or is influenced by their own experience.

Everyone is likely to have questions, sometimes the answers cannot be found until you have spoken to your doctor. Below are some of the most frequent questions that need to be answered:

- Which form of contraception should I use?

- What is the difference between the different types of pill?

- What do I do if I miss a pill?

- Am I likely to forget to take the pill?

- Am I pregnant?

- Do I have to pay for the pill?

- How often do I need to return to my doctor for a prescription?

'Everyone is likely to have questions, sometimes the answers cannot be found until you have spoken to your doctor.'

Of course, there are hundreds of further questions that might be asked concerning the pill – some may be specific to your circumstances whilst others may be more general and borne out of simple curiosity. If you have questions that are not covered in this book, always make a note of them and ask your doctor during your next appointment.

Getting the next prescription

When you first start taking the pill, your doctor may only give you one month's supply at a time for the first three months to make sure it is suitable for you. He or she will want to check your blood pressure and carry out further tests or ask you questions in the initial months, so you may not get a repeat prescription immediately. If there aren't any problems during this initial period, it is likely that you will get a repeat prescription every three months.

Prescription collection

So long as it is a repeat prescription, it is possible to permit someone else to pick up your prescription for you. The documentation must be filled out correctly and the person must sign to say that they are collecting on your behalf and they are not pretending to be you.

The person collecting it will usually be asked to confirm to the dispenser your name and address. Occasionally they may also contact you or your doctor to check and confirm your prescription.

Of course, the easiest way to ensure you are receiving your prescription when you need it is to obtain it yourself. You can simply give the repeat prescription request sheet to your doctor who will decide if you need to be seen or if they are happy for you to continue with the next prescription. This slip can then be collected and taken to a pharmacy in exchange for your medication.

It is normal to expect to see your doctor every six to 12 months when taking the pill to make sure your general health has not been affected. Often this may only require you to have a blood pressure check.

'It is normal to expect to see your doctor every six to 12 months when taking the pill to make sure your general health has not been affected.'

Need2Know

It may also be useful to take advantage of the many prescription collection schemes that are offered to the public. Some chemists will collect your prescription sheet for you and deliver your medication to your home address. Not all pharmacy departments offer this scheme and some only offer it to those who fulfil a certain criteria but there are some who offer the service to everyone.

Allergies and the pill

Many people suffer allergies to medications or other substances and are often concerned that the pill may contain an ingredient that causes a reaction. Those with food allergies and sensitivities, such as those who have Coeliac disease or are lactose intolerant, often express concern over the ingredients in medicines. It is very important to tell the person prescribing the pill or the dispenser if you are sensitive to any ingredients.

At the moment there is only one type of contraceptive pill available to those with lactose or gluten allergies or sensitivities. Etynodiol Diacete (carries the brand name Femulen) is a type of mini pill that is free from both gluten and lactose.

As more and more people are suffering from allergies, manufacturers are constantly trying to create drugs that are safer and can be taken by more people. It may be worthwhile contacting the companies that produce contraceptive pills directly if you're worried.

Changing to a different type of pill

You might find that the pill you have been offered is not suitable. There is usually no problem in requesting a change to a different variety, as long as there are no medical conditions that inhibit this.

As there are so many varieties available, it is reasonable to assume that some types work better for you and carry less side effects than others. Your doctor will be able to change your prescription once you have described exactly how the pill has affected you.

It is recommended that additional contraceptive cover is used during the change over period as your level of protection may dip during this time.

'As more and more people are suffering from allergies, manufacturers are constantly trying to create drugs that are safer and can be taken by more people.'

The pill and interactions with existing medications

As the pill is known to interfere with certain types of drugs, it is very important to tell the person prescribing the pill about any existing medications. Antibiotics are typical in this category, as are some homeopathic remedies and herbal preparations.

Those who are taking drugs for epilepsy or diabetes will need to be assessed so the doctor can find out whether the oral contraceptive will be suitable.

Remember, it is in your best interests to disclose all relevant medical history to the doctor.

Taking the pill and discovering pregnancy

If you are taking the pill and become pregnant, you may not know as early as those who do not use this form of contraception. This is simply because many of the early signs are masked by the pill.

Obviously, the first sign is a missed period, but withdrawal bleeds can still occur when you are on the pill.

Other signs of pregnancy include nausea, vomiting, breast tenderness, tiredness and bloating. If you are suffering from any of these, although it's unlikely if you are taking the pill, you could do a home pregnancy test to either confirm or rule out a pregnancy.

If you achieve a positive result, stop taking your pill and see your doctor for a professional confirmation.

The pill and its effect on an existing pregnancy

For the small percentage of people who fall pregnant whilst taking the pill or those who are pregnant when they first begin to take the pill, there is no reason to worry that the drug has caused any harm to your unborn child or has affected the development of the foetus.

However, it is important to tell your doctor if you think you are pregnant when you ask about the pill as you will need to be aware of your options and book in as an ante-natal patient.

Reaching the menopause and the pill

It is true that the hormonal effects of the contraceptive pill may disguise the usual symptoms of menopause, but it will not be detrimental to your health. In fact, physicians recommend that contraceptive measures are continued for at least 24 months following the onset of the menopause and that you should not have had a bleed during this time. However, when taking the pill, you may still bleed monthly, even after the menopause. This is because these are withdrawal bleeds and not true periods, so you may be unable to tell if you have been period free for this length of time. If this applies to you and you believe that you are almost through the menopause, please speak to your doctor who will advise you on the best course of treatment.

If you think you may be going through the menopause or have finished it, your doctor will be able to perform a simple blood test that will measure the hormonal levels in your blood.

Whilst waiting for these results, it is advised that you continue to use some form of contraception until the menopause has been confirmed.

Summing Up

Even though many people now regard the pill as a common and routinely prescribed medication, the regime that is needed to ensure it works correctly can seem quite complicated at first and may pose lots of questions. The consequences of not understanding the pill properly are very serious, so it is very important that any questions you may have are asked and fully answered – no matter how small or irrelevant you think they might be.

Your doctor will understand your concerns and can provide information about a vast range of subjects. Doctors will also appreciate and respect the consideration that has gone into making decisions about contraception. So, remember, there is no such thing as a stupid question!

Chapter Twelve

The Male Oral Contraceptive Pill

What is the male oral contraceptive pill?

The subject of the male contraceptive pill has been a hot topic for some time. Research has begun on the development of a suitable pill, but as yet it has not been perfected and tested enough to warrant as general release.

There are a variety of male oral contraceptives being researched; some are to be taken in the long term like the female pill and alter sperm production, while other options are to take a one-off pill when anticipating a sexual experience, following which sperm levels return to normal.

In reality, the chances of a male pill that is taken orally are still quite low. Research has now found that men's hormonal contraceptives are more likely to be given as a combination of oral pills taken in conjunction with a series of injections or implants, as opposed to a single oral tablet that is taken daily like the female form.

Why was it created?

One of the main reasons the male pill was initiated was due to the potential huge market value of such a creation. As the use of condoms, a vasectomy or abstaining from sexual intercourse are the only available options, the market place for such a pill was seen to be huge. Offering men more choice allows for greater autonomy over birth control and may be very beneficial for those in a relationship where the female cannot take the pill for medical reasons.

'The subject of a male contraceptive pill has been a hot topic for some years now and researchers are keen to develop a form that is both effective and suitable for the user.'

Another reason is because of the liberation and autonomy it gives males, taking the emphasis of contraception away from the female and sharing the responsibility.

How does it work?

At the moment research trials are being carried out to test the different types of male pills. Many of the earliest forms of the male pill were based on trials that altered the testosterone production and levels in the body as a way of trying to inhibit the production and release of sperm. Initial results proved that this was not a reliable method as many men continued to produce sperm even when the testosterone level had been altered.

Subsequent investigations showed that by using testosterone in combination with progesterone based drugs, contraceptive cover was improved and some of the side effects were prevented. The progesterone, or progestin, temporarily switches off the messages to and from the brain regarding sperm production. However, this fall in sperm production also caused a deficit of testosterone so an injection or implantable form of testosterone was created.

More recent research has shown that altering the levels of a substance called prolactin may be more effective at reducing sperm production. These tablets aim to reduce the production of prolactin and, if used alongside those that alter testosterone, they may significantly impair the production of sperm.

How is it taken?

How to take the male pill depends on the type of pill that is released for general use. Some may require you to take the pill shortly before sexual intercourse whilst others may need to be taken everyday.

As the drugs have not yet been perfected it is difficult to state exactly how they should be taken, what to do if they are not taken correctly and what conditions and medications will alter the function of the drug.

Some men and women have also expressed concern over the reliability and compliance of a man taking the pill and fear that it may not be taken correctly. As a result, experts are also looking at the additional benefits of creating an implantable form of the contraception that is used in a similar way to the female version of contraceptive implant. Further to this, they are exploring some very encouraging results – by using a combination of implants and injections, contraceptive cover seems almost 100% reliable.

Are there any side effects?

Up to now, the side effects that have been discovered from trials show that there may be an increase in mood swings, lower libido and a decrease in testosterone. These findings are to be addressed with further research and when the drugs have been deemed safe for public use, each man enquiring about their use will have all possible side effects explained to them before they are prescribed the pill.

Current availability

There is no male pill available for general use at the moment, but scientists hope that preliminary research will continue to show positive results and that human trials can begin in the next few years.

As there are different companies interested in the male pill it is likely that once an ideal form of the pill has been perfected, the various companies will release different brands of pill based on the available evidence.

It may be possible to enter into trials of the drugs currently being researched; your doctor may be able to advise you on your suitability for the trials and how to look into it further.

When the pill docs become available for general use, it may be helpful to refer to the following checklist before seeking a prescription:

- Can I make the commitment of taking a pill/injection everyday or each time I want to have sex?

- Should I disclose taking the male pill to my partner?

- Am I at risk of an STI?

- Should I also use a condom?

- Do I understand how the male contraceptive works?

- Is it a reliable enough form of contraception?

Summing Up

The subject of a male contraceptive pill has been a hot topic for some years now and researchers are keen to develop a form that is both effective and suitable for the user.

Initial aims were to provide an oral tablet that could be taken either every day or before sexual intercourse, but trials have shown that a combination of hormone injections and implants are the most effective way of providing hormone-based contraception for men.

Although there are no forms of this contraception available for general use in the UK at the moment, it is hoped that research will continue and it will not be too much longer before these drugs are deemed safe and reliable for use by men.

'There is no male pill available for general use at the moment, but scientists hope that preliminary research will continue to show positive results and that human trials can begin in the next few years.'

Additional Information

There are many sources available in modern life that can assist your research on contraception. The UK has numerous agencies that can help provide information or discuss concerns about the pill and any information discussed will remain confidential.

Brook Advisory Centres

Often called simply 'Brook', these centres are a voluntary and national service that offer free and confidential advice on all matters of a sexual health nature and are available to under 25s.

The staff at Brook are often medical personnel who give their time and knowledge, providing a fast, free and effective service to young people in the UK.

They can offer information and advice on all aspects of contraception and will help you make the right decision regarding your own individual contraceptive needs. Any legal or professional queries can be answered and information can be provided either online or by telephone. See the help list for contact details.

Family Planning Association (fpa)

The Family Planning Association is an excellent resource and is available nationally. There are centres up and down the country providing information and advice on any matter regarding your sexual health and contraceptive needs.

They are most often run by local nurses and GPs. The staff know that you are attending the clinic usually because of contraceptive reasons and will have all the information readily available during the sessions.

Most also operate a drop-in service, making it a lot easier for people to visit rather than having to make an appointment in advance.

You will usually be able to pick up some condoms for free at these clinics and be able to find leaflets and booklets that can be taken away if you want to read more at home in your own time.

The Family Planning Association also has a very good website with plenty of information about contraception, as well as contact details and locations of all the centres in the UK. See help list for more information.

Your GP

Your GP will be able to provide a wealth of knowledge and will usually be very up-to-date with current research, trends and will have a strong awareness and comprehension of the vast spectrum of contraceptive pills available. He or she will also have access to your medical notes and will be able to assess any medical history and current complaints that may suggest that one type of pill is more familiar than another, making it easier to select a safe and appropriate prescription for your individual needs.

Along with this, your doctor is highly equipped to recommend other forms of contraception that may be more beneficial to you and your individual needs.

Sexual Health Nurse/Practice Nurse

Often members of the public find it easier to talk to nurses rather than doctors. A nurse will often be able to explain things using less technical vocabulary and can talk patients through things step by step. Practice nurses can be located in your Primary Care Trust through your GP clinic; all appointments will be kept confidential.

The Internet

This is often the first place people look for information these days. It can usually provide many of the answers you are looking for and there are several health-related websites written by professional medical personnel or those with a keen interest. However, there are also those who write articles without having any professional knowledge at all – so be careful!

As there are no laws or guidelines surrounding this subject, many of these websites should be approached with caution as the information they provide may not necessarily explain the true facts or issues surrounding the subject.

NHS Direct

The formation of NHS Direct has provided the public with a safe, reliable and easily accessible form of health information and can be used to find out information regarding healthcare decisions.

When you first ring up NHS Direct you will speak to an operator who will take your details and a brief 'summing up' of your query. This information will then be passed on to the most suitable person who can answer your questions. They will then usually phone you back and discuss your query in greater depth.

Alternatively, you can visit their website (see help list), which contains a vast amount of health information on a wide range of subjects.

Sexual Helpline

As sexual health is such a wide and varied topic and affects so many people living in the UK, there are many special telephone lines dedicated to answering your sexual health questions and providing free and confidential advice.

The staff can advise on all forms of contraception and will help you decide which option is best for you and where you can receive contraceptives.

See help list for more details.

Help List

Brook Advisory Centres

421 Highgate Studios, 53-79 Highgate Road, London, NW5 1TL
Tel: 0800 0185 023 (helpline, Monday to Friday)
Tel: 020 7950 7700 (24-hour information line)
admin@brookcentres.org.uk
www.brook.org.uk
Brook provides free and confidential sexual health advice and services, specifically for young people under 25. Brook has 40 years' experience of providing professional advice through specially trained doctors, nurses, counsellors and outreach and information workers to over 200,000 young people each year.

Contraception Education

135 Victoria Street, Glossop, Derbyshire, SK13 8JF
Tel: 01457 850860
enquiries@contraceptioneducation.co.uk
www.contraceptioneducation.co.uk
Contraception Education provides sex and relationship education resources and training. They promote safe sex, preventing unintended pregnancy and preventing STIs and diseases. Their online shop sells sex education resources. They also run study days, workshops and presentations.

Cool Nurse

www.coolnurse.com
This American site, although still relevant to the UK, is aimed directly at teenagers. It provides lots of information about general health issues, including STIs.

embarrassingproblems.com

info@healthpress.co.uk
www.embarrassingproblems.com
This website is provided by Health Press Limited. It provides lots of 'straight talking' information on a range of personal health issues, including sexual health. Information is also provided on visiting doctors and clinics.

Family Planning Association

UK office
50 Featherstone Street, London, EC1Y 8QU
Northern Ireland
3rd Floor, Ascot House, 24–31 Shaftesbury Square, Belfast, BT2 7DB
3rd Floor, 67 Carlisle Road, Derry, BT48 6JL
Scotland
Unit 10, Firhill Business Centre, 76 Firhill Road, Glasgow, G20 7BA
Wales
Suite D1, Canton House, 435–451 Cowbridge Road East, Cardiff
Tel: England 0845 122 8690 (Helpline, 9am to 6pm, Monday to Friday)
Tel: Northern Ireland 0845 122 8687 (9am to 5pm, Monday to Thursday, 9am to 4.30pm, Friday)
www.fpa.org.uk
This is a free, confidential service offering advice, information and support on making choices about contraception, pregnancy issues, STIs and general sexual health well-being. Visit the website for details of local clinics near you or call the helpline for more advice.

likeitis.org

likeitis@mariestopes.org.uk
www.likeitis.org
This fun site provides lots of information on all aspects of sex and sexual health, including quizzes and an opportunity to ask questions.

Net Doctor

5th Floor, 7 Swallow Place, London, W1B 2AG
www.netdoctor.co.uk
A site covering all aspects of health, with information provided only by
health professionals. Includes an archive of Q&A of everyday problems
and discussion boards on several topics, including the pill. The sex and
relationships section provides information on all aspects, broken down for
men, women and couples.

NHS Direct

Riverside House, 2a Southwark Bridge Road, London, SE1 9HA
Tel: 0845 4647 (helpline)
www.nhsdirect.nhs.uk
NHS Direct provides information and advice about health, illness and health
services, to enable patients to make decisions about their healthcare and
that of their families 24 hours a day. Visit the 'contraception and family
planning section' for information on the combined pill, POP pill and male oral
contraceptive pill.

Patient UK

www.patient.co.uk
Provides lots of up-to-date information on the pill.

Playing Safely

Tel: 0800 567 123 (helpline)
www.condomessentialwear.com
This website was set up by the Department of Health. It includes two gambling
games to illustrate the Sex Lottery and other excellent resources such as
addresses and contact numbers for local GUM and family planning clinics.

R u thinking?

Tel: 0800 28 29 30 (advice line)
www.ruthinking.co.uk
A site for information and advice on sex, love and relationships. Provides particular detail for young people thinking about 'doing it' for the first time. The 'Lad Pad' and 'Lady Lounge' provide perspectives from both sexes. Information is also provided on the pill and other hormonal contraceptives.

Sex, etc.

www.sexetc.org
A website with answers to sexual questions by teenagers and a range of other non-sexual health information too.

Sexual Health

Unit 1, Britannia Court, Moor Street, Worcester, WR1 3DB
Tel: 0800 783 2936 (helpline)
www.sexualhealth.org.uk
A great site covering general information on sexual health with a section on the POP pill and combined pill.

Smarter Sex

www.smartersex.org
This website is all about STIs and sexual health - it provides the facts! There is also a page where you can test your own knowledge of sexual health, so you can see just how much you really know.

Talk Choice

www.contraceptivechoices.co.uk/talkchoice
Talk Choice aims to give women the information needed to start and guide contraception conversations with a doctor (or nurse/pharmacist) and raise their voice for choice! This site gives information on the contraceptive options, including the pill, so women can choose a contraceptive to suit them.

Teenage Health Freak

www.teenagehealthfreak.org
Teenage Health Freak provides web-based, accurate and reliable health information to teenagers in a contemporary, cringe-free, entertaining and informative way.

thesite.org

Tel: 020 7250 5700
www.thesite.org.uk
A site for young people including information on sex, pregnancy, sexual health relationships and much more. Very clear information and very easy to navigate. Email questions through the site.

Women's Health Concern (WHC)

4-6 Eton Place, Marlow, Buckinghamshire, SL7 2QA
Tel: 0845 123 2319 (advice line)
www.womens-health-concern.org
Run by professional nurses and medical advisors, this is both a telephone and e-mail (via an online form) service offering counselling and support to women regarding sexual and gynaecological health.

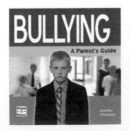

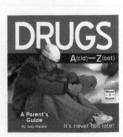